First published 2017 by Mollis Parente

Copyright © Mollis Parente 2017

The right of Mollis Parente to be identified as the author of this work has been asserted by him in accordance with the
Copyright, Designs and Patents Act 1988

All rights reserved. No part of this publication may be reproduced, stored in a retrieval system, or transmitted, in any form, or by any means (electronic, mechanical, photocopying, recording or otherwise) without the prior written permission of the publisher

For permissions contact: mollis.parente@gmail.com

This book is sold subject to the condition that it shall not, by way of trade or otherwise, be lent, hired out, or otherwise circulated without the publisher's prior consent in any form of binding or cover other than that in which it is published and without a similar condition including this condition being imposed on the subsequent purchaser

CONTENTS

INTRODUCTION 3

PART I Where to Begin 20
Chapter 1 - Begin at the End *21*
Chapter 2 - What to Do Next *30*

PART II What to Work On 52
Chapter 3 - A Marathon Not a Sprint *53*
Chapter 4 - Reading *57*
Chapter 5 - Maths *65*
Chapter 6 - English *83*
Chapter 7 - Verbal Reasoning *101*
Chapter 8 - Non-Verbal Reasoning *112*

PART III How to Get Over the Finishing Line 121
Chapter 9 - The Four Month Plan: Week E-13 to Week E+4 .... *122*
Chapter 10 - The Final Stretch: Week E-2 to Week E+4 .... *142*
Chapter 11 - Are We There Yet? *156*

APPENDICES 165
Appendix A - Selection of Practice Books *166*
Appendix B - Suggested Reading List *168*
Appendix C - Interview Questions *171*

INTRODUCTION

1. The most important part

You must understand two things at the outset:

- your child does not need to be tutored to pass an 11+ exam[1]. It is a truism that every year many engaged, hardworking children who have followed the National Curriculum in England will receive offers to join Year 7 of selective schools without the help of an 11+ tutor (whether a selective state school or in the independent sector). That is not to say a tutor cannot be a valuable resource, but you, the parent, need to have clear views on how the tutor's efforts will fit with what your child needs and what *you* will be doing to address these needs.

---

[1] Throughout this book, '11+ exam' means an entrance exam set by an academically selective state school or independent school that is taken in the final year (under 11) of primary school (such as 11+ selective state school exam, 11+ independent school exam or a Common Pre-Test).

- you must remain responsible for your child's 11+ progress. Your child will only sit 11+ exams once, so *you* need to make sure she is ready at the right time for whichever selective school exams she prepares for. If not you, who should be responsible? Do you really believe all those that do not succeed with 11+ exams are either incapable of passing 11+ exams or just late developers? How many of them have not been prepared well enough for these one-off exams?

2. Parental tutoring

While it might look very difficult to combine the roles of parent and tutor to your child, you can certainly do it well. As a parent, it can often feel contradictory to try to protect your child from the stress of the 11+ process, while making sure she is well-prepared for each exam. This book sets out practical steps for you and your child to follow, which will minimise this stress for everyone. These steps range from how to develop the key exam techniques your child will need, to preparing for and attending interviews.

One word of warning: it is most important for parents to be careful that your own actions do not create unnecessary stress for your child on the 11+ journey. Even a sensitive, mature child, who absolutely understands what 11+ exams represent and is keen to do her best, might not feel 11+-related stress with anything like the intensity felt by her parents. If you follow the framework here, this will help you to minimise your fear of the unknown, and keep your accumulated worries away from your child.

3. Mismatched exam timing

The National Curriculum in England obliges primary school children to be tested around May of their academic Year 6. This Key Stage 2 testing ("KS2 SATs") in May Year 6 is the culmination of a child's primary education over the preceding 4 years. It is an important milestone for primary schools themselves (as well as the children), because of their influence on primary school league tables. Since the selective school Year 6 exams do not feed into national primary school league tables, it is reasonable that primary school children will be prepared for KS2 SATs without any regard to the timings of when any selective school Year 6 exams are scheduled.

Unfortunately, selective state schools and independent schools will have completed their Year 7 recruitment process well before May Year 6:

- entrance exams are sat for selective state schools usually in September/October Year 6 and for selective independent schools usually in January Year 6; and

- selective state and independent Year 7 school places are allocated typically by early March Year 6.

It is the vacuum created by this timing mismatch that drives the annual activity of parents preparing their children to peak like athletes earlier in the season for the selective school exams. This mismatched timing means you too need to make sure your child is prepared for the appropriate exam at the appropriate time.

4. Building your child's academic abilities

All that extra time your child spends preparing for 11+ exams is valuable time spent learning and being educated. She is not developing a skill that she will never use again. Instead she will be working hard to improve her academic abilities and knowledge in Maths, English, and logic skills and reasoning (for Verbal reasoning and Non-Verbal Reasoning exams).

In my experience, if your child works to sit selective school exams in September/October Year 6 and January Year 6, this only improves her KS2 SATs results in May Year 6. Without this work, it is of course unrealistic to expect your child to achieve the same level of attainment at the beginning of Year 6 as towards the end of Year 6 in the KS2 SATs. Otherwise what will she have learnt at school during that year?

5. You do not need a tutor for your child

I am a parent but neither a teacher nor a tutor (other than to my children). I believe a tutor can be very helpful to your child in preparing for 11+ exams, but is far from necessary.

- Tutoring can be a useful way for your child to learn and improve exam technique and for her to better understand what to expect from an exam, but as she can learn these important skills in other ways, including from you, a tutor is certainly not necessary.

- Where your child receives a tutor's help, you need to make sure you appreciate how this fits with what she is doing at school. Remember she will spend over 5 hours per day sitting in a classroom for 5 days a week, so is it realistic to believe 1-2 hours a week of tutoring can replace much of the material she is already covering in school?

- Engaging a tutor to help your child to work on weaker areas is quite different to trying to supercharge her exam performance. If you try to supercharge her performance without first ensuring all the basic understanding is in place, you risk making her progress hollow and unsustainable.

A poor reason for using an 11+ exam tutor is because you are suffering from a Fear Of Missing Out. If everyone else within your social circle is using one, you still need to be sure it is the right decision for your child. Plenty of parents push their 11+ child into tutor classes just as a way to Do Something.

Before signing up for any tutor, step back and understand what you expect from the tutor and what are the best ways for your child to meet these expectations.

6. If you want a tutor, how to find a good one

Parents of those preparing for 11+ exams are famously poor at sharing information in case they provide a 'competitor' with any sort of advantage. With schools often attracting more than 1000 applicants for just 100 places, it is very unlikely that withholding information in this way will materially improve anyone's chances of receiving an offer from a school, but I do not expect the secrecy of the school gate to change anytime soon, so you need to do your research well. I have set out in this book how to find a tutor you can be happy with.

In my experience, tutors are often very open with prospective parents and will let your child join a lesson to try them out first. After all, you represent up to 2 years' of potential fees for them, so do try a lesson before you sign up your child. The tutor will most likely see your child individually once a week or perhaps in a class of 10 or more, so find a good tutor that you are comfortable with. Moreover, ask your tutor detailed questions that will give you the information you believe you need to sieve through them, such as:

- how often they test the children;
- whether you will get reports/open evenings/briefing sessions;
- how does the tutor deal with a topic a child is having ongoing difficulty with;
- what materials will they provide; and
- where do the children they tutor go to. Some tutors will be specialists in preparing students for specific school exams as they teach for that type of paper.

Larger 'tutor schools' will typically offer 11+ practise exams during the summer, which are open to all for a fee. These are worth considering if only to familiarise your child with the discipline of sitting in an exam hall surrounded by lots of others sitting their exams. You should confirm you will receive from these schools a breakdown of your child's results benchmarked to everyone else sitting those exams.

Remember that your child will be the one sitting the exams not the tutor, so once your child starts with a tutor make sure you always keep updated on the path and extent of your child's progress. After all, when any tutored child that you know received offers from a range of schools, how many tutors have you ever heard of saying it was all because of the child's effort and practice and actually had very little to do with whatever the tutor had been doing during their time together?

Some tutors use a written exam to select those they will agree to teach, which is quite different to testing your child's progress during the classes. I would keep well away from anyone who tests to select who to teach. A tutor's primary goal must be to develop each particular child to pass the 11+ exams she sits and not merely to teach only those candidates the tutor is already confident will be able to pass the 11+ tests. Otherwise, is this really teaching or just letting your child work hard (and you paying fees) just to bolster that tutor's marketing boast of "...90% of my candidates have received offers from their first choice selective school"?

7. The framework in this book

This book details a framework for parents who want to prepare a child for 11+ exams. If using a tutor is your preferred route, this framework can of course also be used in parallel to your child attending regular sessions with a tutor. At the very least this book will give you a proven alternative path to employing a tutor. Anyway, are you happy to leave this preparation entirely to a tutor, who will after all be paid the same fees whether or not your child receives even a single offer from a selective school?

Part I of this book describes the mechanics of identifying the schools your child will apply to, and an overview of how this will drive your child's preparation and timetable. It also discusses some of the key skills she needs, namely:

- how to practise past papers;

- how to develop good habits around checking; and

- how to improve timing.

Part II of this book describes the key areas that your child will need to address for 11+ exams in each subject, including what needs to be covered and how to answer questions in the following areas:

- Maths;

- English;

- Verbal Reasoning; and

- Non-Verbal Reasoning.

Part III of this book details a 4-month plan to prepare your child for her exams and for the interviews that follow. This plan is then described in daily detail for the final 2 weeks leading up to the first exam and the 4 weeks that follow that date, which will encompass all the exams your child sits and the interviews your child attends.

If I see something pushed into an appendix to a book, automatically this lessens how important I think it is. Consequently I have tried to keep the content of the appendices here focused to a minimum. The appendices here do include:

- selection of 11+ practice books;

- suggested 11+ reading list; and

- selection of 11+ interview questions.

8. Knowing when your child has prepared enough

How do you know when your child has prepared well-enough for an 11+ exam? The simple answer is that you cannot know for sure, but you will see a step change in her approach to, and quality of her answers after, she practices all of these steps. When you see this step change, it is critical she does not then feel she has reached the end of this journey. This is the time she must keep practising all of these steps. In fact, she should not stop her practice until all the exams have been sat and the interviews have been completed.

If you never see this step change before your child sits her exams, you must still keep your child striving to work on these steps (however volatile or disappointing any of her test results might be). **In the end, only the performances in the actual 11+ exams matter; the rest of the papers are just for practice.** Persistent effort and resilience are two of the core qualities you should want your child to keep demonstrating.

9. Using this framework after 11+ exams

Practically, the framework in this book is something your child should continue to use in her future education. Why should your child learn a new framework each time she has an exam to do or moves onto a different level of her education? Much better she refines and adapts the same framework once she has deployed it successfully. In fact, this entire framework is really about putting into practice the following core qualities that underpin so much of 'success' (academic or otherwise):

- persistent effort;

- resilience; and

- empathy.

Persistent effort and resilience are clearly needed to build any important skill over an extended period of time: how can skills be improved without your child continuing to work hard and not giving up. These exam skills and techniques your child is learning are built in the same way.

Resilience is the ability of your child to bounce back from any difficulty she experiences. In reality, resilience is not just a single quality of an individual but more the result of a collection of different strategies and abilities that she has developed over time to work through any problem she encounters, whether that is working on solving Maths problems or resolving issues with her friends.

The important thing to understand and believe is that resilience can be developed by anyone. There is much advice available on how to build resilience, with key principles including:

- developing realistic goals and moving towards them over time;

- maintaining a hopeful outlook, expecting good things and visualizing what is wanted;

- accepting the circumstances that cannot be changed;

- avoiding seeing crises or stressful events as problems that cannot be solved;

- understanding how feelings are affected by difficulties encountered; and

- acting decisively when things do not go favourably.

Perhaps 'empathy' at first sight strikes you as being unimportant. By empathy I mean your child's empathy with other children who work less than your child, learn more slowly than your child or indeed race ahead of your child at school or in tutor classes. Through empathy, your child will appreciate that different children learn at different rates and eventually will have different levels of preparedness for the 11+ exams. Neither how prepared a child is nor how much a child has learned is fixed by her intelligence. Rather the level of preparedness for an exam is more a reflection of a child's degree of persistent effort and resilience of her learning up to that point.

- Just because her friend does badly during one class, does not mean your child (or her friend) should give up on a subject as being too difficult. This is just the time for your child to show her resilience, so that she continues to persist with effort and prepares better next time.

- If your child's friend tells her that boys are good at Maths but girls are not, your child needs to understand through empathy that this is just her friend's perspective and not a universal truth.

Awareness through empathy of the paths taken by others and the views they hold is really quite an appealing way to discuss with your child how important it is to stick with the 11+ process through to the end: all children and adults have their own views, but your child's results will be determined by the work she does or does not do. Then through her empathy, your child will genuinely come to appreciate that her own mistakes and failures too are not set in stone and can often be fixed through her own persistent effort and resilience.

10. Can your child be over-prepared?

I believe it is an unhelpful myth often attributed to some selective school headteachers that you can prepare your child so well that she is accepted by a school where she will struggle once in Year 7. If after all of this a school cannot distinguish an over-prepared child from one showing good potential, then really they should give up as educators.
If over-preparation is a real concern for you, I believe it should help you to know that children are

often interviewed before a place is offered, and that an interview is no longer just about your child going through the motions before receiving an offer of a place (if it ever was). Many more children are typically interviewed for selective independent schools than places ultimately available. In addition to academic ability, intellectual curiosity and genuine enthusiasm for extra-curricular activities are very much desired by these schools, which believe these attributes allow a child to make the most of their secondary education. The interview will typically provide a great forum to showcase your child's abilities and enthusiasms.

PART I
Where to Begin

Chapter 1 - Begin at the End

First things first: begin at the *end* not the beginning. Your child's 11+ journey is a project you need to manage, so begin with the goal of receiving an offer from each school where you are happy to send your child. Then work back to what needs to be covered, when and by whom to make sure you achieve this. You need to plan all of this very carefully.

1. Put together a broad list of potential schools

Start by making a list of which schools does your child/you want to receive offers from. Your child cannot go there unless she first applies to them.

Identifying this initial list will be a seemingly haphazard process, as you find out about interesting schools in your area either through word-of-mouth or in published information. At this investigative stage, do not be tempted to rule out schools that are a bus ride or train journey away as many schools look for pupils from a large catchment area, so they often arrange a spaghetti of coaches to draw in the pupils they are aiming to attract. Obtain information from wherever you can sensibly draw it from, including school websites, Ofsted inspections and Independent Schools Inspectorate inspections. Also, look at the destinations of leavers from primary schools in your area over the past 3 or more years (and prep schools, if you have access to that information too).

2. Narrow this list to your preferred schools

Once your broad list of potential schools is settled, you should obtain a copy of each school's prospectus (or download this from typically helpful school websites). Then arrange to visit each school on its 11+ open day or arrange an individual visit if you miss the 11+ tour. (Independent schools often also offer 'school in action' mornings and perhaps workshops that your child could join. These are all worthwhile to signup for to get a better feel for what a school offers.)

Many parents and children attend these days at the end of their child's Year 5 as a first step in gathering this information or even at the beginning of Year 6, but I believe Year 4 is the best time to start this process. By May Year 5 use all of this and other information you locate to move from your broad list to a more focused narrow list by removing those schools you no longer want to pursue and adding others to your list if you find them attractive. Narrowing your broad list to a narrow list of 4 schools will ensure your child has plenty of exam practice, but without swamping her under too many school applications. Update your narrow list with the latest information on these schools available at the end of Year 5.

It is sensible to apply for a spectrum of potential schools but each of these should be where your child might feasibly go, as otherwise you are wasting your money on unnecessary registration fees.

3. School application timetables

Each school typically publishes annually an application timetable for prospective pupils setting out all the key steps to sitting its 11+ exam. These timetables include application deadlines and application dates for scholarships and bursaries. (At this stage, keep an open mind about these scholarship and bursary dates as your circumstances could well change before your child sits 11+ exams, and there is no real benefit in ruling out these potential paths right now.)

Locate the latest admissions timetable for each of the schools on the narrow list. Call each admissions office to understand what changes, if any, are expected to its 11+ process, and how you can obtain an updated timetable.

When you receive a final copy of this year's admissions timetable for a school on your narrow list, complete a copy of Table 1.1 below using these details. This allows you to collect all of this logistical information in one place. It will be important later. In particular, you need to note when this narrow list of schools will set their exams in Year 6.

Often selective state schools run their exams in September/October Year 6 (with some areas testing as early as the first week of September with a short window to register in May of Year 5), with independent school exams usually taking place in January Year 6. If selective state schools are important to you, then it does not help your child to be prepared to sit 11+ exams only in January Year 6, i.e. 3 months after the selective state schools set their exams. In contrast, if your child is ready to sit exams by September/October Year 6, it is relatively straightforward to keep her prepared by practising the same skills until she also sits selective independent school exams in January Year 6.

For each school on this narrow list, make a note in your copy of Table 1.1 of all the exam papers your child will sit. While the exact combination of papers will depend on each school, they are likely to be 2 or more papers from the following:

- Maths;

- English;

- Verbal Reasoning; and

- Non-Verbal Reasoning.

Table 1.1. Summary of information collected on your narrow list of schools

School	Open Day Date	Application Deadline	Application received by School on:	Scholarship / Bursary Deadline	Scholarship / Bursary Application received on:	11+ Exam Papers to Sit

4. Keep all options open

Typically in the autumn term of Year 6, local authorities in England close school applications for September Year 7 entry ahead of announcing state school place allocations in the early part of March Year 6. Each local education authority runs its own admissions process based on bespoke criteria, so it is critical you are familiar with the timings of all the processes and deadlines that might affect your child both for selective state schools and non-selective state schools.

For the local authority secondary school transfer process, you need to have identified which non-selective state schools your child should apply to attend in Year 7, and sieved these through the familiar process of attending open days, reviewing Ofsted reports and questioning teachers at these potential candidates. In parallel to your child's 11+ exam preparations, you need to make sure you keep track of your local authority secondary school transfer process, even if you are only planning to use it as an option of last resort. If your child's circumstances in September Year 7 mean she has to attend one of these schools, you should make sure now that you and she understand what you have signed her up for.

Remember that, however well-prepared your child is, there will be no guarantee that your child will be accepted by any of the selective schools she will sit exams for. While understandably you want to focus all of your energy on the 11+ process, your first priority must be to make sure your child has a school to go to in September Year 7.

It is beyond the scope of this book to provide any further guidance on non-selective school entry processes, except to say again how important it is not to forget your child does need to have at least one school to join in Year 7.

5. Choosing the school

Once your child has completed all of her exams and interviews, she will find out in late February / early March Year 6 which independent school and state school places she has been offered. You will usually have 2-3 weeks to make your choice, so use that time to think through the options, including visiting the schools again to help your decision-making.

As a child can only attend one school even if she has received 4 offers, all the other offers have to be rejected. This will open those places to the next children on each school's waiting list, which means it is quite possible that by the end of March Year 6 your child might receive an offer from a school even if initially she was put on its waiting list - although I have never heard of a rejection being converted into an offer during this period.

6. Next steps

You have now mapped out which schools your child will apply to and the exams she will prepare to sit at each school. The next Chapter gives an overview of how your child should get ready to sit the selection exams set by each school.

Chapter 2 - What to Do Next

1. Explain to your child why she will do this

Does your child know what the 11+ exams are for and why she will be working so hard for them? Is it just because you tell her to? You should take time to explain to her what will result from her 11+ work, including:

- allowing her to join the particular schools you identified together in Chapter 1. Your child is intelligent enough to understand that working hard will give her more choices of schools, and this discussion will of course be easier if the prize is a school place that she really wants.

- boosting her preparation for a good performance in the KS2 SATs.

Your child understanding this could be the difference between (i) you having to cajole her throughout the 11+ process, and (ii) she understanding you are going to help her reach her goals, but ultimately it is her time this will occupy and all of the benefits will accrue directly to her, so she must make the effort to work hard.

Path (ii) is certainly the better way for you and your child, as I do not believe path (i) is sustainable: if your child needs to be pushed through every step, there will come a time, perhaps after she has started at *your* dream school when she will feel lost or will simply rebel when there is no longer anyone standing over her making sure she continues to put in effort – say, around the time she is 12 or 13 years old, I would expect. Ultimately, her drive to get through the 11+ process will need to come from her, especially if she is to take the lessons and benefits of this process to build on in future exams and tests.

Even if your child happily accepts being spoon-fed during her entire school career, what about when she reaches university? Why would she then suddenly develop the capacity to set and work towards her own goals? Of course it is not impossible this could happen, but surely it must be easier for someone to set and achieve goals by confidently redeploying a trusted framework that she has used before over a number of years, rather than each time she wants to pursue a goal she has to find and rely on someone she trusts to direct her?

2. When to start the 11+ journey

Many tutors recommend beginning 11+ exam preparation in January Year 4. Why such a long time before the exams? The theory behind this is, I understand from different tutors, it takes this long to make sure your child is up to speed and fully prepared to sit 11+ exams in the different subjects.

I am not convinced that there is real value in attending classes with a tutor from January Year 4, as the past papers practised at this time will be Year 4 level (for ages 8-9), and so are of course nowhere near as difficult as an actual 11+ paper. Nor are the Year 4 level practice papers easily built on in Year 5 and Year 6: your child will not yet have been taught the Year 6 (for ages 10-11) and Year 5 syllabuses, which form the basis of 11+ exam papers.

Neither do I believe the discipline itself of practising papers in Year 4 helps to develop the valuable timing skills or good checking habits needed for the 11+ exams. Again, those skills are best practised by using papers similar to the 11+ exams that will actually be sat rather than just *any* timed paper.

However, during Year 4 you must make sure your child is comfortably grounded in all the basics of

English and Maths that a Year 4 child is expected to have covered by focusing in particular on her weaker areas, so, for example, she should:

- know her times tables;
- know how to spell words that the National Curriculum in England advises she should be able to;
- be able to write creatively in sentences and paragraphs; and
- understand how to approach comprehensions.

If she can't yet do these things, you need to help her practice to build and consolidate these skills, which will support the work your child's class teacher will be doing.

Consequently, and assuming you see the need to employ a tutor at all, I believe January Year 5 is a better time to begin classes with a tutor, but by then your child should already have been reading widely throughout Years 4 and 5, and practised some commercially produced papers then to begin to understand the elements of exam technique and to highlight her weaker areas.

Part III of this book outlines a 4-month plan, which in my experience is the **minimum** time you will need to prepare your child for her 11+ exams.

3. Motivating your child for the 11+ process

I believe a child learns best if she works hard with an open approach. What do I mean by an open approach? I mean she must be open to believing her hard work will build her knowledge and skills, and allow her to make valuable connections between them. She must believe her success and growing abilities are fundamentally driven by how hard she is working rather than because she is intelligent. She must believe that what she can achieve is not driven by talents that she has been hardwired with from birth. She must believe the powerful idea that her 11+ results will reflect the amount of high-quality, resilient effort she puts into this process.

4. Dweck's growth-mindset

My personal experiences and views on the importance of a child having an open approach I see reflected in the 'mindset' work of Carol Dweck,

Professor of Psychology at Stanford University in the US. Dweck's central belief, developed by her extensive research over her long academic career focused on psychological motivation and development, is that a child's success is not determined by innate talents and intellect. Instead, Dweck believes, a child's success depends upon the child's mindset regarding each of her qualities, e.g. the child will be more successful the more she believes she has the capacity to grow her intelligence through her own hard work. But this mindset approach could apply just as well to an individual's other qualities, such as creativity and athleticism, and the degree to which these other qualities can be developed.

Dweck explains that all individuals can be placed somewhere on a spectrum based on their personal views of where their intelligence and abilities come from.

- Some believe their success is based on abilities they are born with. These are said to have a 'fixed-mindset'.

- Others believe their success is based on hard work, learning and persistence. These individuals are said to have a 'growth-mindset'.

Dweck defined fixed and growth mindsets in a 2012 interview:

"In a fixed mindset students believe their basic abilities, their intelligence, their talents, are just fixed traits. They have a certain amount and that's that, and then their goal becomes to look smart all the time and never look dumb. In a growth mindset students understand that their talents and abilities can be developed through effort, good teaching and persistence. They do not necessarily think everyone's the same or anyone can be Einstein, but they believe everyone can get smarter if they work at it."[2]

Individuals might not even be aware of the mindset they have regarding a particular quality, or indeed that their mindset might change depending on what others say to them or the stories they tell themselves. However, their behaviour in different situations will indicate the mindset they hold. This is famously indicated by the reaction to failure:

---

[2] "Carol Dweck on the Growth Mindset and Education". *OneDublin.org*. 2012-06-19.

- fixed-mindset individuals have a fear of failure because of their belief that failure permanently defines you as a loser. This produces a need in these individuals to prove themselves over and over again, with a consequent refusal to take risks in case that behaviour leads to their failure. This fixed-mindset, Dweck explains, results in their belief that only untalented individuals have to work for success and making an effort somehow diminishes them as individuals. Therefore, as they are talented and intelligent, they believe, and they cannot change these qualities through hard work, they ought to succeed at tasks merely because they are talented and intelligent. So they will avoid taking on anything risky and risk failing, as this will highlight, they believe, the limits of their talents.

- in contrast, growth-mindset individuals do not mind or fear failure to the same degree because they realize their performance can be improved with effort and practice, and learning comes from making mistakes and productive failure. A growth mindset will promote an individual's:

- willingness to work hard to achieve success;

- love of learning; and

- emotional resilience.

This means an individual with a growth-mindset is more likely to continue working hard and be encouraged to continue despite any setback she experiences (i.e. she will show good resilience).

5. Parent can build and support a growth-mindset

Further, an individual's effort level can be altered just by how parental praise influences the mindset she might develop:

- a child praised with "well done, you are very clever" is more likely to develop a fixed-mindset to avoid circumstances where she might not look clever; but

- a child praised with "well done, you worked very hard" is more likely to develop a growth-mindset that builds on her hard work.

So, what should a parent do to develop a growth-mindset in a child?

- When your child succeeds, focus on the work and effort she put in to gain that success. Emphasise this is what she needs to do the next time too.

- Praise her persistence and perseverance. Focus on the good habits your child practised and the choices she made that lead to her success.

- Expectations you have of your child should focus on her good habits and effort in developing a skill or building knowledge, not the outcome of grades or passing 11+ exams.

- If there is any failure, your child should see what she learns from the experience and what she could try to do things differently next time. Do not blame others.

- Do not focus on your child's past mistakes and perceived shortcomings other than to work with her to develop strategies to improve weaker areas.

- Weaker areas need to be addressed with concrete plans rather than with vague statements to your child like "You must try harder".

- Explain how you use a growth-mindset to deal with challenges and to continue to learn.

- Do not label yourself in ways that demonstrate you have a fixed-mindset ("I was always terrible at Maths").

6. Adapting this framework beyond 11+ exams

The framework set out in this book (including the detail of Part III) is designed to be adapted by your child as she grows older, so that it can form the basic scaffolding for your child's revision for future exams and building towards other goals. These might include Year 7 exams, GCSEs, A levels and your child's degree course. Moreover, your child can only study now not yesterday or in the future. This means the way for your child to realise a long-term goal is for her to work hard *today*.

Of course a degree course's content is far richer and deeper than anything to be covered for the 11+ exams, but I believe it is important for you to appreciate (and perhaps even recognise within yourself) the benefits of applying this book's approach to future exams rather than discard it now only to need to reinvent this particular wheel later. The essential steps to exam success will always be these:

- Begin by setting out a detailed timetable so that your child can cover everything needed in the time she has available. She should not try to do all of her revision in a few days. By pacing her studies, she will avoid being overloaded with information and feeling burn out. This underlines how important it is to have a well thought out revision timetable. She should discipline herself and get into the habit of revising regularly and sticking to her timetable.

- It is important that she uses past papers and syllabuses to work out what she should be revising. She should not waste time on topics that are not relevant for the exams. In later exams, she will also need to base revision on textbooks and her written notes.

- Go over material more than once, but she should leave a day or 2 in between. This will help her to reinforce knowledge in her mind, and setting aside time for breaks from the work is very important to allow her brain to consolidate what she is learning.

- If things are not going to plan, she should not panic. Just think again about what can be covered in the time remaining, and focus on what she can feasibly achieve in this time.

7.   First step of the 11+ journey

Make sure your child joins the local lending library (ideally before Year 4). See Chapter 4 below for more on reading to prepare for the 11+ exams.

8.   Steady progress is key

Remember that over time you must encourage and develop steady improvement of your child's performance. Your child cannot do this all in one day and neither should she be discouraged by occasional backward steps. If that happens, identify the questions where difficulties are occurring (and hence the weaker areas), then address these one question at a time. It is useless just to tell your child "It is not good enough" or "Just get it right".

Unless your child's lack of improvement is solely because of a deliberate lack of effort by her, you can only improve her performance by addressing problems one question at a time.

If a lack of improvement is because of a deliberate lack of effort, you must decide honestly if your child will put adequate effort in even if she is accepted at a selective school.

9. Practise past papers

As a parent, you must take real care not to obsess about the scores your child is getting while practising past papers during this process. You should also act to avoid your child fixing on them in any way, at least until they start to show good improvement. Even then your child's emphasis should be on developing and refining her strategies to build a body of improving test scores, i.e. developing and honing checking skills (these are certainly skills rather than in any way innate) and building concentration (by working productively or reading thoughtfully for up to an hour at a time).

Go through each practice paper straightaway after you have marked it to address the problem areas identified by each question your child has got wrong. Make sure you work through each of these questions to show your child how to do them. This revisiting difficult areas is the learning process in action: you need to actually do this for every question not just for a sample or the ones you believe are most difficult. Every question. This should be done slowly by walking through the structure of each answer, so your child remembers the method the next time she sees a similar question. In fact, always try to relate any question you discuss with your child to another question you have already come across – even in another subject if you believe that is a useful connection to make.

10.   Improve exam technique

You need to keep explaining to your child about exam technique, which she will in time understand

and develop. Remember, at aged 10 she will not have developed yet the exam experience you might have gained from sitting many exams over a number of years. Your child needs to be told what to expect from a serious exam, which might well be quite different to her experiences of class end of year tests. Discuss with her what to expect and describe she will be expected to do in each exam.

- Carefully read the instructions at the beginning of an exam.

- If your child gets stuck on a question, she should move on and come back to that question at the end if she has time. Sometimes perseverance with a question does pay off, but it is crucial your child has the overriding understanding that sitting an 11+ exam paper is in essence showing her knowledge through 3 key skills, which, in order of how these skills need to be developed, are:

    o **accuracy**: collecting marks accurately wherever she can throughout an exam paper. This means there is no benefit to her in spending all of her time to produce only one perfect answer. This is the skill of harvesting marks by learning to judge when to persist with a question and when to move onto the next one. She will develop this through practising past papers.

o **checking**: methodically and diligently checking her work as she goes through her response to a question. She is unlikely to have sufficient time at the end of an exam to re-engage with every question, i.e. she will not have enough time to work through the paper twice. This is the skill of wringing out a few more marks from a paper, which could be the difference between beating a pass mark or not. When you review with your child a completed practice paper, the questions where checking would have added a few more marks are often glaringly clear, and I would encourage you to highlight to your child on each paper the difference between the actual score achieved and what would the score have been if your child had checked it more carefully. Checking is the skill it took me longest to persuade my children was extremely worthwhile for them to spend time on.

What this skill is not really about is 'intelligence', but instead understanding that a 'mark' is a 'mark', whether it is obtained by answering a question correctly or checking and correcting a wrong answer to regain a mark that would otherwise have been lost.

- **timing**: your child must get used to collecting marks and checking her work while remaining aware of time pressure of the exam. The best way to develop this skill is to practice a range of papers under timed conditions. Even after practicing a particular style of paper 3 times, you will see a strong improvement in your child's speed without her needing to sacrifice accuracy. Then she needs to keep improving her speed by continuing to practice under time pressure, but do not allow your child to sacrifice accuracy for the sake of speed (supported by her checking), i.e. she must work to improve speed only after she has been accurately collecting marks and diligently checking.

- When your child attempts a question, she must read it slowly and carefully to make sure she understands it. She must comprehend clearly what the question is demanding. Your child must then consider:

- what question has she seen in the past that appears to be like this? How is this question different?

- what will the form of the answer look like?

- what are the steps she will need to complete to be able to produce a finished answer?

- how to mentally 'tick off' the different bits of useful information that can be leached from the text of the question to move towards an answer.

- once she has set out a well-structured answer with each step clearly described, how to go through each step again to check that the arithmetic has been done correctly and check if her answer is inconsistent in its logic or presentation.

- that she should check again that the answer she has written actually answers the question that has been asked.

Initially it will take time to develop these skills, so they should be done very slowly and carefully, but your child will get faster with practice, especially when she starts recognising the correct steps she will need to follow for even novel questions.

Eventually, just by looking at a question, she will be able to mentally map an answer to a Maths question just as she will be able to scribble an essay plan before beginning to write an English composition.

11. Keep a diary

Keep a diary to record outline information on each practice paper sat by your child:

- the paper's name;

- the date it was sat;

- the score and percentage achieved; and

- short notes on any real areas of difficulty highlighted by that paper.

Over time this diary will form the core of your approach to address your child's weaker areas, so make things easier for yourself and ensure you add full information on everything your child is doing without including too many shorthand notes that you might not understand in a few weeks' time.

As the whole 11+ process is about being systematic, it is critical that you have the most accurate information available to you on how your child has learned different concepts throughout the process and the paths that have been taken successfully to improving checking and timing skills. Relying just on your memory to direct your child's 11+ preparation is not enough, as your memory will not be good enough - no matter how photographic you think it is.

The information in your diary will be critical to what you ask your child to do and when, especially during the final 6 weeks of her 11+ journey that stretch from the final 2 weeks before her first exam to the 4 weeks after then. (Chapter 10 discusses the detail of what you need to do during this period.) I cannot stress highly enough that you must not lose this diary.

12. Next steps

This Part I set out useful background to the skills to practise over time as your child moves towards the date of her first exam. Next, Part II describes which subjects and materials need to be learned and practised to prepare your child to sit her 11+ exams.

PART II
What to Work On

Chapter 3 - A Marathon Not a Sprint

Now that you have an understanding of the timings and 11+ subject exams to be set by your selected schools, you must be clear on what material needs to be covered to prepare for any exams in Maths, English, Verbal Reasoning and Non-Verbal Reasoning. This Part II describes:

- where to begin with each subject;

- how you should cover the materials examiners use to form questions; and

- how your child should approach these exam questions, so that she picks up as many marks as she can.

The key to covering this material is to work through it all carefully to understand which areas your child is very comfortable with and which areas require more effort from her, especially paying attention in your diary to understanding her weakest areas. You can then help her spend more time to tackle the weakest areas first. It is no good your child reviewing only the material she is already comfortable with, while hoping the other material is not examined. It will be.

Working on the gaps in her knowledge will also help your child to contextualise better the whole of a subject, e.g. understanding percentages in Maths will also help her understand fractions and proportions better rather than if percentages, fractions and proportions were learned as 3 unrelated areas each in its own silo. In any exam question that offers the prospect of picking up a meaningful number of marks, individual topics will not be examined in isolation, but rather a good understanding of their relationships will be needed to give a complete answer.

Your child cannot cover all of this material in a few days, so make every hour of your child's time count by practising these skills and knowledge over time. Steady progress is key as this is a marathon not a sprint, whether that is when you and your child are working according to the 4 month minimum timetable described in Part III or have started earlier.

Before you focus your child on learning and improving her exam technique, first make sure all the material has been covered well. Remember that it is best to go over the material more than once to consolidate knowledge in your child's mind (and she will know the material better if you go over it at least 3 or 4 times). Where there is limited time left until the exams, it is even more important to cover each topic carefully and efficiently before moving onto practising past exam papers, otherwise you will have to use up valuable practice time later to instead go over these materials again from scratch.

The following subjects are covered in the remaining chapters of this Part II:

- ***Reading***: reading independently is the bedrock of your child's 11+ journey. This will teach her vocabulary, and develop grammar, comprehension and concentration skills, as well as build her bank of general knowledge. Reading is unlikely to form a separate exam, but is a very important component of comprehension in each of its forms below.

- ***Maths***: these 11+ papers test comprehension of basic Maths and arithmetic techniques, particularly in the form of 'word' questions. Simple arithmetic sums will also have to be completed accurately.

- *English*: all of these 11+ papers involve either testing comprehension or composing creative writing pieces. The key here is to teach the structures your child will need to use to answer each question well.

- *Verbal Reasoning*: these papers assume your child has a very good understanding of English language grammar, spelling and extensive vocabulary. These questions will require your child to use comprehension skills to answer them, together with reasoning and logic. In many ways this is the analogue to English language as Non-Verbal Reasoning is the analogue to Maths.

- *Non-Verbal Reasoning*: these 11+ papers are based on comprehension and reasoning around visual presentation of problems and information. This subject demands your child is comfortable looking at sequences of pictures, shapes and numbers, and although these are unlikely to be based directly on mathematical operations, they often require confidence with Maths in that they are based on pattern-recognition and searching for visual and logical connections.

Chapter 4 - Reading

a) Where to begin with reading

We must begin with reading, which is absolutely core to all of your child's learning during Years 4, 5 and 6, as well as beyond. It seems hardly a week goes by without some new study affirming the strong connection between reading and academic attainment, and some are unequivocal in concluding children who read for pleasure are likely to do significantly better at school than their peers[3].

Ideally, reading will have been a real focus for your child ever since she started at school (if not before), but it is quite possible that your bright, engaging, conversationally-able child still has no real desire to read independently. If this is the case (more likely, but certainly not exclusively, if your child is a boy), it is not too late to address this to prepare well for the 11+ process.

---

[3] See CLS Study below in this Chapter.

1. Reading is critical for 11+ exams

Understanding the importance of reading is a good starting point to help develop your child's reading skill. It is not just about reading words and trying to connect them to make sense of a sentence. This is just the start.

Reading should be active: the reader needs to connect the text being read to her own general knowledge and past experiences to derive as much meaning from a text as she can to comprehend its context as well as the content. Confident, experienced readers learn to do this all quickly without consciously focusing on each step, and they appreciate that reading is always a search for understanding and meaning. However, many children never realise that reading is more than just learning to pronounce words and building vocabulary, so they never build their reading skill to a point where it boosts their academic performance in different subjects.

A Centre for Longitudinal Studies (CLS) study[4], which claims to be the first to examine over time the

---

[4] Sullivan, A. and Brown, M. (2013), Social inequalities in cognitive scores at age 16: The role of reading. CLS Working Paper 2013/10.

impact of reading for pleasure on cognitive development, found that children who read for pleasure made more progress with their Maths, vocabulary and spelling when aged 10-16 years old than those who read rarely. In fact, the combined effect on a child's academic progress of often reading books, visiting the library regularly and reading newspapers at age 16 was estimated to be 4 times greater than the advantage children gained from having a parent with a degree.

2. Difference between a good reader and a poor reader

I believe the core of the difference between good readers and poor readers is the difference in the total amount of time they spend reading.

I expect your child already spends a dedicated, albeit relatively short, 30 minutes at school each day reading. With your child's time outside the classroom already filled with extra-curricular activities, homework, TV and being online, it might seem there is little time for her to squeeze in reading time. However, reading more each day at a regular

London: Centre for Longitudinal Studies

time will quickly develop her reading skills, so that soon she searches automatically for comprehension and meaning whatever the form of text in front of her. Reading is a skill that develops quickly with practice, and it demands developing the reader's concentration. It is far from being an innate talent.

Reading actively across a wide range of material will help your child build stronger connections between the different strands of knowledge she discovers. The wealth of possibilities this gives her will drive her on to read more for comprehension and meaning, and encourage her independent thinking.

Practically, a confident reader preparing for 11+ exams needs to be able to:

- use the 'gap' strategy to work out the meaning of unknown words. This means your child should read over the unknown word (i.e. treat it as a blank space) and then think about words that could fit in that gap but still make sense within the context of the relevant preceding sentences and those following.

- read according to punctuation and grammar, which drives reading for meaning.

- read aloud with good expression.

- understand and interpret imagery and structure of poetry.

b) How you should cover this

1. Developing your child's reading skills

In my experience, if there is no real love of independent reading by Year 4, then you will need to *insist* on your child reading for a daily half an hour, which she should build to a full hour each day by the beginning of Year 5. If you leave it until later to act, this will only make it harder to impose the disciplined task of building up this time to one hour of reading each day. Yes, *impose,* because reading is that important to education in general and the 11+ preparation in particular. After all, if all 11+ exam questions are comprehension or composition, how will your child comprehend nuance in descriptive Maths questions if she is not yet reading well enough.

Once your child reads for an hour for a few days (and this must be 5-6 days per week), it is important then she always reads out loud. Why? Because otherwise it is easy for her to skip over any seemingly difficult word without learning its pronunciation, although she might well still recognise it by sight. This vocalization also helps improve her learning a new word, as hearing herself pronounce a word then fixes the form of this in her mind (and indeed how this compares to you voicing the word). If it is an unfamiliar word, she must also look up its meaning right away in a dictionary. When later she meets any of these words during her sub-vocalised reading of comprehension passages in practice papers and exams, this initial vocalisation will help her recall the pronunciation and meaning of this word. Sub-vocalisation is believed to help integration of past concepts with those currently being processed by a reader, i.e sub-vocalisation will help to contextualise a new idea into the mind of your child as she reads a novel passage.

She might have questions or even say she understands everything, in which case quiz her on the different elements she encounters during this reading to keep her thinking about what she reads: once comfortable with verbs, nouns, adverbs and adjectives, she should move on to identifying, for example, prefixes and suffixes and how these affect the root of a word, then meaning of imagery and idioms, etc.

If at first during reading aloud her progress seems achingly slow, bear with it but stick to the amount of time you and your child have committed to (i.e. 30 minutes building to an hour daily). This is the stage where she *should* be taking things very slowly and reading for long-term understanding.

2. Extended reading builds exam concentration

Reading is also a great way for your child to build and demonstrate her ability to concentrate on one task for a whole hour, which is particularly important because 11+ exams are typically up to 1 hour each. Try to cover this reading at the same time each day but not as part of the bedtime routine.

Let your child know it is no more than one hour and she will continue to do it, perhaps not always willingly at first, but take care not to exhaust her by asking her to build her reading above 1 hour.

c) Preparing for the 11+ exams

What should your child be reading to help her to prepare for the 11+ exams?

In Appendix B I have set out a selection of books that will help your child build reading confidence, vocabulary and general knowledge.

I always told my children it is important to finish a book even if they decided half way through it was not interesting (and they needed to read at least 5 chapters before even being allowed to say that). When in your job or preparing for exams have you only read what interests you? Much more likely that you have had to plough through turgid prose because you were needing to read for good comprehension. It is another important discipline for the 11+ journey, as well as beyond.

Newer technologies, such as e-readers, can also offer easy access to books and newspapers and it is important that you continue to encourage your child's reading, particularly in her teenage years after 11+ exams are only a distant memory.

Chapter 5 - Maths

a) Where to begin with Maths

What is the Maths your child needs to know to prepare well?

1. Learning Maths or arithmetic?

Your child must understand that to answer any Maths question will likely involve applying more than one set of techniques:

- there are a collection of different mathematical techniques that she must learn over time, so that she develops a very good sense of when to deploy them and in which combination: this is **Maths**.

- if she then needs to actually work out a number as an answer, there are a further set of techniques that she must use: this is **arithmetic**.

I believe it is helpful for you to think that Maths is driven by comprehension and creativity, while arithmetic is principally about rote-learned facts, accuracy and checking. This distinction might strike you as artificial and possibly unhelpful, especially as Maths still needs to be accurately checked. However, I believe it is a critical starting point, which will help your child improve her feel for knowing when it is appropriate to use Maths techniques and when to use arithmetic techniques.

2. Key topics to address

Start by teaching Maths based on some key concepts:

- multiplication is repeated addition (e.g. 3 x 2 means '3 lots of 2', which is 2+2+2 = 6).

- division is repeated subtraction (e.g. 8/4 means 'how many times can 4 be subtracted from 8', which is 2, i.e. 8-4-4=0).

- use 'counting on' to turn subtraction problems into addition sums, which will produce a better understanding of what is going on in subtraction problems: 9-5=4, which means counting on from 5 to 9 is 4.

- describe what fractions represent and how they relate to proportions/ratios (e.g. 1/8 means 1 part out of 8).

- word questions in Maths and arithmetic are essentially exercises in comprehension. Just trying to remember facts will not help your child answer word questions very well. She needs to understand how numbers relate to other numbers. This will then help her develop her intuition about what feels right (and what does not) about how numbers relate to one another. However, times tables do need to be learned well, so that your child can recall them straightaway as otherwise she will not make connections between numbers quickly enough if all her effort and time is spent on *calculating* times tables.

Key areas that you should cover with your child ahead of the 11+ exams include those needed to answer questions drawn from the following topics:

- Place value (i.e. key is to identify quickly where the decimal point is located)

- Multiplying/dividing by 10/100/1000 (i.e. multiply by moving the number to larger columns, and divide by moving to smaller columns. The decimal point never moves)

- Fractions (vulgar): using mixed numbers / equivalent fractions / cancelling

    - **ADD**:
    $$\frac{1}{3} + \frac{1}{4} = \frac{1 \times 4}{3\ 4} + \frac{1 \times 3}{4\ 3} = \frac{4+3}{12} = \frac{7}{12}$$

    - **SUBTRACT**:
    $$\frac{1}{3} - \frac{1}{4} = \frac{1 \times 4}{3\ 4} - \frac{1 \times 3}{4\ 3} = \frac{4-3}{12} = \frac{1}{12}$$

    - **MULTIPLY**:
    $$\frac{1}{3} \times \frac{1}{4} = \frac{(1 \times 1)}{(3 \times 4)} = \frac{1}{12}$$

    - **DIVIDE**:
    $$\frac{1}{3} \div \frac{1}{4} = \frac{1}{3} \times \frac{4}{1} = \frac{(1 \times 4)}{(3 \times 1)} = \frac{4}{3}$$

- Fractions (decimal): adding, subtracting, multiplying and dividing fractions

- Converting vulgar fractions to decimal fractions to percentages, and combinations of these

Fraction	Decimal	Percentage
1	1.0	100%
4/5 = 8/10	0.8	80%
3/4 = 6/8	0.75	75%
2/3 = 4/6	0.66	66.66%
5/8	0.625	62.5%
3/5 = 6/10	0.6	60%
5/10 = 1/2	0.5	50%
2/5 = 4/10	0.4	40%
3/8	0.375	37.5%
1/3 = 2/6	0.33	33.33%
1/4 = 2/8	0.25	25%
1/5 = 2/10	0.2	20%
1/8	0.125	12.5%
1/10	0.1	10%
1/20	0.05	5%

- Percentage increase / decrease

- Percentage / ratio / proportion

- Highest Common Factor / Lowest Common Multiple

- Prime numbers / Square numbers / Cube numbers

- Median ("the middle number when lined up in order"), mode ("the MOst popular") and mean ("the other 'average'")

- Data and graphs

- Naming 2D and 3D shapes

- Calculating perimeter, area and/or volume of different shapes

- Converting units

- Symmetry (line and rotational)

- Angles (e.g. triangles in a polygon to give sum of interior angles)

- Approximation / significant figures

- Time: 12-hour and 24-hour clocks

- Basic algebra with up to two variables

- Exchange rates and different time zones. These questions are best approached by answering the following to structure an answer:

- o "Where are you sitting, and where are you imagining the other person is located?"

- o This emphasises visualizing the question and then 'seeing' a drawing of the answer, rather than relying on memorized facts that might or might not be applied correctly to answer a question (such as applying exchange rates).

- Practising word questions

- Relevant vocabulary:

    - o **SUM** of 3 and 2 is 5; **SUM** of 2 and 3 is 5

    - o **DIFFERENCE** of 3 and 2 is 1; **DIFFERENCE** of 2 and 3 is (-1)

    - o **PRODUCT** of 3 and 2 is 6; **PRODUCT** of 2 and 3 is 6

- **QUOTIENT** of 3 and 2 is 3/2=1.5; **QUOTIENT** of 2 and 3 is 2/3

b) How you should cover this

Firstly, I truly believe that anyone can learn Maths; it is really about your child having an open approach to the subject. With this sort of approach, she must understand Maths is fundamentally about making connections to support carefully set out logical reasoning. Make sure your child sets out her working fully, because this makes the reasoning much easier to follow and speeds up her checking process.

Keeping in mind Dweck's research from Chapter 2, I believe people with a growth-mindset tend to do better in Maths than those with a fixed-mindset. If you believe you are smart, and you struggle on a task, you are likely to decide the task is actually too difficult for everyone if a smart person like you cannot find the answer. Then you are more likely to give up rather than push on with the task and succeed by persisting with the struggle. (Remember, a fixed-mindset is associated with believing you should not need to struggle with a task if you are clever.)

If instead you believe that you can learn anything and determined effort is an important part of everyone's learning process, when you struggle, you will keep going to try and find the answer. You are then more likely to find the correct solution to the question precisely because you persist.

You will also find that the range of questions included in past papers will typically depend on the type of school setting the exam. For example, selective independent school Maths papers often increase in difficulty as the paper progresses, and they will usually throw in 2 or 3 questions at the end of a Maths paper to test the skills of the most able, whereas the focus multiple choice questions set by selective state schools is often more focused on accuracy and speed.

1. Developing a good feel for Maths

With making and understanding the connections between different Maths and arithmetic techniques, your child's feel and comfort for numbers will get better as she will begin to see that where she thought there was only one way to answer a question, there are often other ways to do so.

Your child should expect there will often be a number of quite different ways to answer a Maths question, but her persistence and hard work will uncover and connect a broad set of successful approaches, e.g. she will see just by looking at 6-3 that the answer is 3, but might be slightly less comfortable seeing that 52-49 is 3, even though it is essentially the same sum. She will probably have spent more time at school on the number bond 6-3=3 than 52-49=3, so she will be more confident to feel that she 'knows' the answer for the former sum.

But what if you asked her the answer to 282-279? She could approach this in different ways, including:

- writing out this subtraction sum using the column method to deduct 279 from 282 (i.e. carrying over from the Tens column to the Units column);

- counting on from 279 to 282 (i.e. "+1" to move from 279 to 280, then move "+2" to move from 280 to 282, which means the difference is +3),

but it is clear here that the counting on method is much quicker than writing out the column method (important when under time pressure in an exam).

Whenever there is time pressure, I always advocate calculating a subtraction sum by counting on rather than using the column method; when counting on is your child's preferred subtraction strategy, she will certainly get faster and faster rather than waste time setting out the column method when there is no advantage in doing so. Of course, an exam question might ask her to use the column method explicitly, so she still needs to understand that subtraction technique well.

2. Knowing more strategies builds a robust understanding

Further, knowing at least 2 subtraction strategies will improve your child's comfort with numbers (and allow an alternative route to checking an answer produced by one of the methods) by not making your child believe she needs to rote-learn one technique and then wheel it out at every sight of a minus sign.

Knowing more than one strategy will build her confidence and skill in Maths, and it will give her a sense that there is robustness in her armoury to deal with, in this case, subtraction problems; a growing security with using numbers in different ways to get the same result will demystify numbers further and build her Maths skills.

The alternative of only knowing one strategy (i.e. the column method) to answer a subtraction sum risks making your child feel the column method is a reliable lifeline, but without her understanding why or ever having the option to use a quicker approach to save time in an exam. If she learns to always first ask why to use a particular Maths strategy, then your child will connect different techniques and develop her judgement of in which situations it is appropriate to use an alternative technique to answer a question.

3. Learning from mistakes really is critical

Your child must also believe it is fine to make mistakes as she learns Maths, but it is very important she tries hard to learn from these mistakes, perhaps not necessarily at the first time of asking but certainly over time. Mistakes will provide her with valuable information on any approach she is taking at any given time and how this can be developed to improve her Maths skills. After all, the framework in this book is both about her getting ready for the 11+ exams at the right time, and to follow an approach to learning that will leave her with a stock of good habits that she can call on throughout her secondary and tertiary education and then into her career. Learning from her mistakes will underpin all of these stages for her.

4. Understand better by drawing the answer

Another important way to build her comfort with Maths and arithmetic is to ask her to draw out her understanding of word questions. This will provide another perspective alongside comprehending a question's words. For example, if your child does not understand the meaning of times tables and just relies on memorising the tables of numbers, this will not help her develop any real feel for them, e.g.:

- if a word question describes 3 fields that each contain 12 sheep, this should be written, because this is what she understands it to mean:

    o 3*12, i.e. 3 fields of 12 sheep in each field, or 3 lots of 12

    o this is 36 sheep in total

- if a word question describes 12 fields that each contain 3 sheep, this should be written as and understood to be:

    o 12*3, i.e. 12 fields of 3 sheep in each field, or 12 lots of 3

    o again, this is 36 sheep in total but their arrangement is very different.

Understanding what the arrangement looks like in each case will let your child answer a supplementary question more quickly, e.g. 'What is the total area of the fields in each case if each field is a square of side 10 metres length?'. If she cannot draw the arrangement then she will need to interrogate the text of the word question to look for clues about which times table fact needs to be used to answer the particular supplementary question.

Relying just on rote-learned facts will fragment understanding of Maths and make it more difficult for her to use them to reason the correct answer, because she will be grasping for which arithmetic sum needs to be calculated rather than understanding the correct reasoning needed to answer a particular question by using Maths techniques. However, your child does need to be able to recall her times tables quickly and well, as well as understand what the times tables mean. Quicker recall of times tables facts will come to your child through using them regularly, and practising speed tables (i.e. timing how quickly your child can complete random grids of times tables) is also an excellent way to develop recalling random sums, so that she will be able to apply them quickly in an exam.

5. Understand better by explaining aloud

When your child has answered a practice question, ask her to explain it to you out loud. If she has answered it correctly, the discipline of walking through the answer will cement the approach in her mind. If she is incorrect, then you can see which step she reached before the problem occurred, and how much of the rest of the problem she could have answered but for the one or 2 steps she did not make the connections to.

c) How to answer Maths exam questions

For each Maths question, your child must:

1. Read the question carefully and, if possible, draw a picture of what is happening. A picture will help to:

    a. gather together what information is available in the question; and

    b. give your child a good mental picture of what is missing but needed to be deduced to answer the question.

2. Using Maths techniques, set out the carefully reasoned answer to the question.

3. Set out the arithmetic sum that needs to be calculated.

4. Calculate the arithmetic sum.

5. Write the answer in the space provided on the exam paper or answer sheet.

6. Check steps 2-5 carefully to make sure:

a. your child has chosen and worked through the Maths methods correctly;

b. calculated the arithmetic sum correctly; and

c. has actually written down the answer she meant to write.

Chapter 6 - English

a) Where to begin with English

What is the English your child needs to know to prepare well?

Your child will need to demonstrate she has a very good command of a number of aspects of English, including:

- reading to understand meaning;

- writing accurately and fluently to communicate meaning;

- writing legibly;

- planning, drafting and editing her own writing; and

- accurately using punctuation, grammar and spelling;

- developing a broad vocabulary through reading a range of genres; and

- proofreading her work.

1. Reading

Reading is the absolute bedrock for 11+ exam success. I really cannot emphasise this enough (see Chapter 4 above).

2. Writing

Learning to appropriately structure a piece of writing will be key to helping your child produce interesting, mature, description-driven writing in an exam. Your child must develop strategies to compose and structure pieces of writing by planning, revising and proofreading for spelling and grammar. Her writing must be directed by:

- a strong awareness of the audience she is writing for;

- what she is trying to achieve with the writing (e.g. is it 'persuasive' or 'informative'?); and

- using a good knowledge of vocabulary and grammar to make her writing's meaning clear.

Overall, your child must be keenly aware of the effects her writing creates, especially to feel that she is able to express clearly in writing the ideas she wants to discuss and to set out the structured reasoning behind these ideas. It is not enough to teach your child a few complicated looking stock phrases that she can write down in all circumstances. She must be able to understand the effects her writing creates. This is very important for the 11+ exams and will continue to be so in future.

3. Grammar, punctuation and spelling

Make a list of the key areas that you need to address with your child. At a minimum these need to cover the following:

- Spelling words correctly and *avoiding* rules like "i before e except after c".

- Apostrophes (i.e. only for possession or to show a letter has been missed out).

- Commas: use this (a) to separate 3 items or more in a list, or (b) to indicate a pause in a list.

- Colons: use this before an explanation, example or a list.

- Semi-colons: use this to (a) separate items in a list, or (b) connect 2 closely-connected independent clauses in a compound sentence.

- Quotation marks for direct speech:

    o Jenny asked, "How is your meal?"

    o "The goulash is wonderful," said James.

- Paragraphs: use (a) for a collection of sentences around one theme, and (b) for direct speech of a new speaker.

4. Building vocabulary

The biggest challenge will be if your child's vocabulary is relatively limited, especially if there is only a short time left before sitting 11+ exams. Within a *very* short timeframe there is not a great deal that you can do, but if your child agrees, you can create vocabulary flashcards and practise these as many as possible each day. In particular, focus on weaker areas, rather than strengthening her stronger areas. As always, the key is to build connections to what your child is already comfortable with and knows, which her attempts at the practice tests should continue to highlight.

5. Proofreading

Every child is told the importance of proofreading, but often finds it very difficult to do - something which adults often share. Why is this? I do not believe children are reluctant to proofread just because it is boring (which of course it is), but rather because it means more work from identifying and then correcting their own errors. After all, if you do not proofread, you cannot find any errors you might have made, which means your child does not need to spend any time correcting them.

Even more than this, I believe proofreading is really avoided by children because all it is highlighting the writer's mistakes, which I am sure not many people like to admit. All you can do is make your child feel it is fine for her to find her own mistakes and correct them as no-one will be able to write a piece under exam conditions (or indeed answer a Maths question) knowing absolutely she has not made any mistake.

Also, it is very important that your child appreciates that if she finds an error, that is one fewer error that the examiner can find, so checking is extremely valuable.

How to proofread? Your child must work through her own checklist that covers many of the errors she often makes and are relatively easy to spot, so that she uses her limited time in the most useful way. Ideally she should aim to correct her errors as she writes, so that she improve the chances of her getting it right first time:

- check that each sentence starts with a capital letter and ends with a full stop.

- when using speech marks, remember for each New Speaker use a New Line for a New Paragraph.

- punctuate direct speech properly (e.g. where to place a comma).

b) How you should cover this

1. Key elements

Your child needs to understand and use in her creative writing compositions and reading comprehensions a number of key elements:

- Knowledge of *words* will help your child use familiar words and techniques to develop a feel for the meanings of unknown words (and so extend vocabulary), and build her knowledge of, for example, key synonyms, antonyms, homonyms and homophones.

- *Sentences* are created by using words with knowledge of grammar (such as of different word classes such as nouns, verbs, adjectives and adverbs) and punctuation (e.g. effects of correctly using different punctuation, such as apostrophes and punctuating direct speech).

- Different types of *texts* are structured to create different effects for different audiences (e.g. the effects of different techniques used in a newspaper article are to achieve something different to effects used in a sonnet), how plots and characters might develop in stories to create different effects, and writing being built up as a process of planning/structuring, drafting and proof-reading.

- *Meaning* in a piece of text is created by how individual words (vocabulary and spelling) are put together in sentences to build compositions (by correctly using grammar and punctuation). A reader can then comprehend what is being said, as well as why particular techniques are appropriate to be used to write in a particular style.

    o Teach spelling and sentence structure in the systematic way of putting together building blocks. Similarly, teach grammar in a way that highlights the effects it creates in a reader.

    o Discuss with your child how meaning in a piece of writing is created using these techniques, or how a film's story arc and character development contributes to the themes the writer/director is discussing.

2. Comprehension

For Comprehension questions, your child should follow a structure like this:

1. Read through all the questions quickly to understand the general tone of what is being asked and the split of different types of question.

2. Read the comprehension passage *twice*:

    a. first, read the passage silently with a pencil guiding the reader; and

    b. then read again while 'mouthing' the words, i.e. sub-vocalise while moving your mouth silently. (This might feel silly to your child, but it will help her (sub-vocalised) comprehension.)

3. Answer all the multiple choice questions that typically appear at the beginning of these tests.

4. Answer all other questions with full sentences, and do not start any sentence with a connective. An answer should be in the

following format (and provide more points, evidence and explanation where a question is offering more marks for a fuller answer):

a. **Point**: answer the question ("Yes, she is a wise woman.");

b. **Evidence**: set out a relevant quote from the passage giving a line reference for that quote, e.g.

    'Firstly, she explains there are some things which an individual is not able to control "…sometimes the cookie crumbles" (line 8).

    Secondly, her neighbour describes the advice she gave him "…the greatest remedy for anger is delay."'

c. **Explain**, i.e. describe how the Evidence supports the Point, e.g.

    - "This shows …";
    - "This indicates …";
    - "This points to …"; or

- "This suggests ...".

5. For questions that demand understanding an unfamiliar word, the most useful strategy is to 'read over' the unknown word (i.e. treat it as a blank space) and then think about words that could fit in that gap, but still make sense within the context of the relevant preceding sentences and those following.

3. Composition

For Composition / Creative Writing questions, your child should follow a structure like this:

1. Take 5 minutes (but try to eventually reduce this to 3 minutes – it is all valuable exam time) to set out a **framework** plan: (i) how the story will begin, (b) the general path it will follow, and (c) how it will end.

2. Better to write good description rather than plot-driven stories. There is only limited time to write in an exam and talking about emotions, feelings, atmosphere, and visual and aural description will give more scope to show writing ability and techniques, than the

scope offered by a plot-driven story. Your child might be concerned that nothing is happening in her creative writing, but actually a descriptive composition will produce a more impressive piece of writing showing a more mature approach and content.

3. What if the mind 'blanks' and she cannot think of anything to write in an exam? Your child needs to practice techniques to brainstorm during writing the plan, which will get easier with even a little practice, e.g. by writing down ideas that are suggested or associated with the title.

Once she has understood that the initial goal is to plan a framework every time, she will manage to do this on demand after some practice. Of course, each framework is really just a vehicle for a piece of descriptive writing and the content is provided by the images she can draw on from her experience and broader knowledge, as well as from her key lists of words and phrases, to support:

- Description (e.g. adjectives and adverbs she will have noted during past writing tasks and discussing situations) and <u>Imagery</u> (personification, metaphors and similes): while it is difficult to have too much description, beware of swamping the examiner with too much imagery.

o Use interesting connectives and subordinate clauses. Interesting <u>connectives</u> to use include:

ADDING	**COMPARING**	**QUALIFYING**	**SEQUENCING**
and	similarly	however	after
also	equally	although	next
too	like	unless	then
as well as	in the same way	except	meanwhile
in addition to		if	firstly, secondly, …
		as long as	… finally

EMPHASISING	**ILLUSTRATING**	**CONTRASTING**	**CAUSE AND EFFECT**
particularly	like	whereas	because
especially	including	instead of	so
above all	such as	alternatively	therefore
notably	for example	otherwise	as a result
	for instance	unlike	consequently
	this indicates	on the other hand	thus
	this shows		
	as shown by		

o Brainstorming the <u>planning</u> can be accelerated by imagining the impact of the title on the 5 senses (i.e. to discuss <u>external</u> triggers of thoughts) and feelings/emotions (i.e. to discuss <u>internal</u> triggers of thoughts).

- o Do not forget the importance of getting the basics right, i.e. verb tenses, spelling, punctuation and grammar.

4. Always spend the final 6-7 minutes checking as you will pick up a number of mistakes. No-one sets out to make a mistake, so it is a safe assumption that your child will find at least some errors, which the examiner will give credit for correcting and also means the examiner then will not find the corrected errors. This will make your child's writing more engaging and impressive.

c) How to answer English exam questions

For each English question, your child's approach will differ for Comprehension questions and Composition questions.

Comprehension

1. Read through all the questions quickly to understand the general tone of what's being asked.

2. Read the comprehension passage **twice**:

    a. first, silently with a pencil guiding your eyes; and

    b. then read again while sub-vocalising.

3. Answer all the multiple choice questions.

4. Then answer all other questions with full sentences, with each answer following this format (and providing more points, evidence and explanation where a question is offering more marks for an answer):

> a. **Point**: answer the question.
>
> b. **Evidence**: set out a relevant quote from the passage giving a line reference for that quote.
>
> c. **Explain** how the Evidence supports the Point.
>
> 5. For questions that demand understanding an unfamiliar word, use the 'gap' strategy to 'read over' the unknown word (i.e. treat it as a blank space) and then think about words that could fit in that gap, but still make sense within the context of the relevant preceding sentences and those following.

Composition

For more **descriptive** answers:

1. Use the first 3 minutes to <u>set out a plan</u> for your writing <u>that you then follow</u>.

2. This plan should allow you to write 5 paragraphs of 5-6 sentences with a beginning, middle and end. It can use the following structure:

    a. Introductory paragraph to 'set the scene': here include lots of description based on:
        i. Your senses ('external')
        ii. Your feelings and emotions ('internal')

    b. Beginning of the story (1 paragraph). Use varied description and imagery.

    c. Middle of the story (2 paragraphs). Use varied description and imagery.

      d. Resolution of the story (1 paragraph). Use varied description and imagery.

      e. Key is to make your child question why she is using a particular literary device and the effects she is using it to create.

3. Leave 6-7 minutes at the end to check through spelling and grammar. This is crucial to make sure the writing is presented in the best way.

For more **plot-driven** stories:

> Use the first 3 minutes to <u>set out a plan</u> for your writing <u>that you then follow</u>.
> This plan should allow you to write 5 paragraphs of 5-6 sentences with a beginning, middle and end that has a story arc.

Chapter 7 - Verbal Reasoning

a) Where to begin with Verbal Reasoning

What is the Verbal Reasoning your child needs to know to prepare well?

Verbal Reasoning exams are about comprehension of written words and language, then reasoning with these to solve problems. They are designed to test a child's ability to understand and reason with words, and, like Non-Verbal Reasoning, they are expected to be more a test of skills, rather than of learned knowledge, although I believe it is pretty difficult to do well with Verbal Reasoning exams without having learned a large vocabulary.

Many of the underlying skills your child will use for Verbal Reasoning are those she uses during English lessons and assessments, including comprehension, spelling, grammar, punctuation and vocabulary. From her wide-ranging reading, your child will learn antonyms and synonyms, homophones and homonyms, and anagrams and other patterns in words.

Verbal Reasoning as a subject is not something your child is likely to have encountered before 11+ exams, so the first step is to introduce her to different types of questions. There are 21 types of Verbal Reasoning questions ("VR Question Type" or "VRQT") that are often used in the 11+ process, each of which will need to be recognized and answered accurately and quickly by your child. These are summarised in section (c) of this Chapter below.

Ask your child to complete a couple of Verbal Reasoning papers, so you can begin to understand the level she is working at. You can then track her progress from this level. Remember, improving understanding is key at this stage and timing is something to work on later, so right now let her take as long as she wants to answer these questions. Make sure you then review each question with her individually (whether answered correctly or wrongly), taking care to ask her to describe how and why she answered each question in the way she did.

Then spend more time on her main areas of weakness, but also continue to do some questions on the stronger areas too.

As well as language-based questions, your child will also need to complete Maths-based Verbal

Reasoning questions that demand a good understanding of Maths operations, such as word/number codes (VRQT 7 and VRQT 19), number series (VRQT 11), Maths equations (VRQT 17) and using reasoning to find the middle number by using the outside numbers (VRQT 18) (see section (b) below).

b) How you should cover this

It is important to ensure that your child has extensive practice and testing in all 21 VR Question Types and any other areas that fall under the title of Verbal Reasoning.

VR Question Types include:

- **VRQT 1: Insert a Letter**
  In these questions the **same** letter must fit into **both** sets of brackets, to complete the word in front of the brackets and begin the word after the brackets.
  Example: col (*) ear bir (*) oll
  Answer: d (cold, dear, bird, doll)

- **VRQT 2: Two Odd Ones Out**

Three words are related, find the 2 words that do *NOT* go with these 3.
Mark them *BOTH* on the answer sheet.
Example: football rugby ball post basketball
Answer: ball post

- **VRQT 3: Related Words**
  The alphabet is here to help you with these questions. You need to work out a different code for each question
  Choose the correct answer and mark it on the answer sheet.
  A B C D E F G H I J K L M N O P Q R S T U V W X Y Z
  Example: If the code for FOUR is IRXU, what does ILYH mean?
  Answer: FIVE

- **VRQT 4: Closest Meaning**
  Find TWO words, one from each group that are the CLOSEST in meaning.
  Mark BOTH words on the answer sheet.
  Example: cold pepper red chilly hot
  Answer: cold, chilly

- **VRQT 5: Hidden Word**
  In each of the following sentences a FOUR letter word is hidden between 2

words. The 2 words will always be next to each other. Find the pair of words and mark them on the answer sheet.
Example: The pig ate everything he could.
Answer: pig ate (gate)

- **VRQT 6: Missing Word**

  The word in capitals has had THREE consecutive letters removed, without changing the order of these letters they will make one correctly spelt word. The sentence must make sense. Find the 3 letter word and mark it on the answer sheet.
  Example: Her BHER cried all night.
  Answer: ROT (bROTher)

- **VRQT 7: Letters for Numbers**

  Letters stand for numbers. Work out the correct answer to each sum. Mark the relevant LETTER on the answer sheet.
  Example:
  A = 7, B = 5, C = 2, D = 3, E = 10
  What is the answer to the sum, written as a letter?
  A - C + B = ?
  Answer: E

- **VRQT 8: Move a Letter**
  One letter from the word on the left can be moved to the word on the right, to make TWO new words. The letters must not be rearranged.
  Example: tripe sir
  Answer: t (ripe and stir)

- **VRQT 9: Letter Series**
  A B C D E F G H I J K L M N O P Q R S T U V W X Y Z
  The alphabet is given above to help you. Find the pair of letters that will continue the series in the most sensible way. Mark the appropriate pair of letters on the answer sheet.
  Example: PE NG LI JK HM
  Answer: FO

- **VRQT 10: Word Connections**
  Find TWO words, ONE from each set of that will complete the sentence in the most sensible way. Mark BOTH words on the answer sheet.
  Example: **Red** is to (face strawberry den) as **Green** is to (grass leaf kiwi)
  Answer: strawberry kiwi

- **VRQT 11: Number Series**
  Find the number that continues the sequence in the most sensible way. Mark the missing number on the answer sheet.
  Example: 0 3 8 15 24 (*)
  Answer: 35

- **VRQT 12: Compound Words**
  Find one word from each group that together makes one correctly spelt word. The letters must not be rearranged. The word from the first group will always be used first.
  Mark BOTH words on the answer sheet.
  Example: (saddle horse pear) (cart some man)
  Answer: horseman

- **VRQT 13: Make a Word**
  Find the word that completes the second group in the SAME way as the first group. Mark the word on the answer sheet.
  Example:
  team (them) they
  snow (*) crop
  Answer: crow

- **VRQT 14: Letter Connections**
  A B C D E F G H I J K L M N O P Q R S T U V W X Y Z

The alphabet is here to help you with these questions. Find the letters that will complete the sentence in the best way.
Mark BOTH letters on the answer sheet.
Example: ST is to UR
as DE is to (*)
Answer: FC

- **VRQT 15: Reading Information**
  Example: Miss Blue, Miss Green and Miss Purple all left work at 6.00 pm. It took Miss Blue 35 minutes to walk home, 15 minutes longer than Miss Purple. Mr Green took 25 minutes longer than Miss Purple to get home. If the above statement is true, only one of the following statements is true.
  A. Miss Blue arrived home after Miss Green.
  B. Miss Green took 20 minutes longer to arrive home than Miss Purple.
  C. Miss Purple arrived home 25 minutes after Miss Green.
  D. Miss Blue arrived home at the same time as Miss Green.
  E. Miss Blue arrived home before Miss Green.
  Answer: E

- **VRQT 16: Opposite Meaning**
  Find TWO words, one from each group, that are the most OPPOSITE in meaning.
  Mark BOTH words on the answer sheet.
  Example: (sunny hot water) (steam windy cold)
  Answer: hot, cold

- **VRQT 17: Complete the Sum**
  Find the number that will complete the sum correctly. Mark the missing number on the answer sheet.
  Example: 32 - 18 = 12 + (*)
  Answer: 2

- **VRQT 18: Related Numbers**
  The numbers in each group are related in the SAME way. Find the missing number and mark it on the answer sheet.
  Example: (2 [6] 3) (4 [32] 8) (12 [(*)] 5)
  Answer: 60

- **VRQT 19: Word-Number Codes**
  In these questions there are 4 words. Three of the words have been given a code. The codes are not written in the same order as the

words. Work out the correct answers and mark then on the answer sheet.
Example:
star seat east
5713 1378 1573
What is the code for EARS?
Answer: 5781
What does the code 3578 mean?
Answer: TEAR

- **VRQT 20: Complete the Word**
  Find the word that completes the third pair of words in SAME way as the first 2 pairs. Mark the appropriate word on the answer sheet.
  Example: pram (map) gripe (pig) good ((*))
  Answer: dog

- **VRQT 21: Same Meaning**
  One word from the answer sheet will go equally well with BOTH pairs of words. Mark the appropriate word on the answer sheet.
  Example: (helicopter, jeep)
  (aquarium, pond)
  Answer options: lake gun cannon tank stream
  Answer: tank

Although this subject involves a different set of question types to Maths and English exams, Verbal

Reasoning is still essentially about comprehension and accurate checking.

Once your child has understood how to tackle the different VR Question Types, she must practise. As you would expect, your child will do better as she practices more. Start this practise by giving your child one or 2 GL Assessment tests. The actual 11+ exam papers will be harder than these, but these tests are a good introduction to a variety of question types and approaches. You can buy these online (see Appendix A). Also, do not forget to explain to your child how a verbal reasoning question should be answered differently to an English question or a Maths question.

Your child might well score highly on these tests straightaway, in which case you should begin encouraging her to check her answers more carefully to squeeze out a few extra marks from each paper, and discuss with her how important it is to check her answers. Otherwise keep going through the question types, then start on practice papers to continue to build accuracy. This is a marathon after all.

Chapter 8 - Non-Verbal Reasoning

a) Where to begin with Non-Verbal Reasoning

Non-Verbal Reasoning exams aim to assess how a child uses her understanding and interpretations of pictures and shapes to solve problems: your child needs to use reasoning and logic to solve problems without using words and language. They are more an indication of Maths ability and associated powers of reasoning than the language-based approach needed for Verbal Reasoning exams. The Non-Verbal Reasoning papers tend to contain a few different question types within one exam, requiring skills such as:

- identifying relationships between objects;

- seeing similarities and differences between shapes and patterns;

- completing picture sequences; and

- testing spatial awareness skills.

b) How you should cover this

Your child's basic approach to Verbal Reasoning questions should carry over to Non-Verbal Reasoning questions, by which I mean:

- Non-Verbal Reasoning is not something your child is likely to have encountered before, so introduce her to different types of questions. Give your child one or 2 GL Assessment tests as an introduction to a variety of question types and approaches. You can buy these from where you buy Verbal Reasoning papers, often from the same publisher.

- Once your child has understood a spread of question types, and you have explained to her how to approach answering them (do not forget to explain that a non-verbal reasoning question should be answered differently to an English question or a Maths question), she will need to practice selections of different types. These different types of questions can be sourced from books such as those set out in Appendix A.

- Your child should spend more time concentrating on her main areas of weakness, but also continue to answer some practice questions on the stronger areas too.

- Build up to encouraging your child to check her answers carefully on each paper to squeeze out further marks.

The different types of Non-Verbal Reasoning questions are typically based on Maths concepts such as rotation, symmetry, consistency/differences in shapes and finding the next element in a sequence. These questions are usually presented as 5 or so diagrams to choose an answer from rather than as word questions.

The best way to start is with actual questions (see Appendix A for suggested Non-Verbal Reasoning books of practice papers for different age groups). Once your child has spent time looking at 3-4 Bond-type papers, she will start recognising and developing her approach to different types of questions. Unfortunately the range of Non-Verbal reasoning questions is much broader than the 21 question types often used for Verbal Reasoning. These question types include:

- Spotting the odd shape out in a *group* (e.g. a 3-sided shape in a group of 5-sided shapes).

The shapes are unlikely to be straightforward, so take one part of the first shape (such as how one part is shaded) and see how this appears in the answers. If there is not an odd one out suggested by this process, take another part of the first shape and compare it to the potential answers. Repeat until a plausible answer is identified.

- Working out what a cube net will look like when it is folded. Remember, 2 sides separated by a square cannot touch, so rule out the answers where they do touch and work from there to visualise how the net would close.

- Identifying the mirror image of a given shape. Draw in on the shape what the mirror image should look like, then look at each answer in turn to see which answer looks just like what was predicted.

- Working out the next diagram in a sequence (for example a series of rectangles divided into squares, where the first has one square shaded, the second has 2, the third has 3, and so on). For this style of question, work out the rule to predict the last in the sequence by:

- thinking of a rule to move from the first to the second answer;

- applying this rule to predict the third in the series:

    - if the third in the series is predicted correctly by this rule, then use this rule to predict the fourth in the series; or

    - if the third answer is not predicted by this rule, go back and find another rule that predicts the second in the series from the first element. Then apply this new rule to see what it predicts the third in the series to be. If this new rule works, then use it to predict the fourth; if it does not, go back to the start and try again.

- Finding 2 identical shapes in a series of 5 shapes. Start by comparing the first shape with each other shape in turn. If identical shapes are found, then write this down as the answer. If none are identical, start with the second shape and compare it with the third shape onwards. If none are identical, start with the third shape and go through the same process. Continue until the pair is found.

- Identifying what a shape would look like when rotated by 90 degrees. It will help to physically turn the paper through 90 degrees and see what it looks like.

- For code questions and more complicated series questions, your child will need to find the general rule first but there might actually be 2 (or more) rules, so it is very important each rule is identified separately, since trying to identify all the rules simultaneously will not get to the right answer in a way that you can then check by reapplying the rules in a different order.

Once your child is comfortable tackling a broad range of different question types, she must practise, as Non-Verbal Reasoning skills will also improve with practice.

Your child should begin by attempting untimed papers then as her scores improve to a high level, she should attempt whole papers under timed conditions. Remember, timing is initially not as important as understanding, so in the earlier stages allow your child as long as she needs to complete these questions. You will soon see which question types your child might be finding difficult and which she is able to speed through.

It is key that your child approaches each question in a disciplined and systematic way: she must look at each element in a sequence in turn to rule out options as she moves through each question rather than flitting backwards and forwards across a question.

c) How to answer Non-Verbal Reasoning exam questions

For each Non-Verbal Reasoning question, your child must:

1. Read the question carefully.

2. Work through each element in the sequence systematically to rule out options as you go along until you are left with only 1 or 2 options, then pick what you think is the best answer.

    a. **Be accurate.** Understand exactly what is being asked and work methodically and quickly to finish as many of the questions as possible.

    b. **Draw the answers.** Draw out what you think the shape will look like once it is rotated or reflected, or draw the part of a figure missing to help you see the answer.

    c. **Attention to detail.** Pay attention to everything on the paper in the question: count the number of sides are there in each shape, angles, colours, shading, line thicknesses, wavy or straight lines, sizes of different elements, rotations, reflections, and anything else that looks like a feature of a shape. That way you can decide what is the same and what is different about the sequence. It is all about spotting the small details in Non-Verbal Reasoning questions.

3. Review the remaining 1 or 2 options again to decide the option that best answers the question.

4. Check to confirm:

    a. your reasoning for choosing this answer still makes sense; and

    b. you have written down the answer you had meant to, i.e. you did not make an error during writing on the answer sheet.

PART III
How to Get Over the Finishing Line

Chapter 9 - The Four Month Plan: Week E-13 to Week E+4

From Part II you will now have a good sense of what needs to be covered for each of the 11+ subjects your child might be examined on, and how to answer the sort of questions she will meet in these papers. This Part III describes how to draw together all of these strands ahead of the scheduled exams.

1. When to start preparing for the 11+ exams

When should your child start to prepare? I have described above that many tutors recommend starting with them at the beginning of Year 4, irrespective of whether your child is preparing to sit selective state exams in early Year 6 (September/October) or selective independent school exams in mid Year 6 (January).

So how will you make sure your child is prepared to sit 11+ exams at the right time? After all, you have probably never done this before, so how can you be confident of getting this most important of timings right? Let me start by describing what I did, which is fairly typical of the approach of many parents that have been through this.

2. My experiences of using a tutor

A - Using a tutor

When I first started my older child on the 11+ journey, I began by engaging a well-regarded local tutor and then leaving everything to him regarding preparing for the 11+ process. I reasoned that he would prepare my child well given the tutor's many years of experience, which his marketing materials described with quotes from parents praising him. I was confident of being able to teach the 11+ exam techniques to my child, but I believed I was paying the tutor 2 years of fees to access the tutor's considerable experience and (hopefully) well-developed judgment, since he had prepared so many children in the past to pass 11+ exams.

My child started with this tutor in January Year 4 and finished with him in December Year 6, i.e. as long a period as any tutor I have heard ask for. Throughout these 2 years, my child spent up to 4 hours at home each Saturday morning through to lunchtime working through a paper a week from a Bond-type or similar book of practice papers for each of Maths, English, Verbal Reasoning and Non-Verbal Reasoning, as well as a seemingly never-ending set of crossword books to build vocabulary. This was work that my child did and I had to mark and review with my child, as this fell outside what the tutor agreed to do. On top of this, my child joined a class of 10-12 children that the tutor ran once a week for 2 hours. During this class, the tutor did look at the list of Bond-type papers completed at home during the previous week, but this review was extremely light-touch judging by the weekly feedback, which was never more than just a bland 'Good work' without any further comment.

The message was clear: my child needed just to keep ploughing on with the various Bond-type books she worked through. I saw that my child's preparation was just like preparing for any exam I had ever sat: by working through past papers and questions methodically, my child was building frameworks of knowledge and techniques that she then connected consciously by using different structures to answer questions in the past papers. By learning more techniques and structures for answers, my child was able to answer more and more questions confidently, accurately and quickly. Ultimately this process was all about working through Bond-type practice papers to build connections between different topics and fill-in gaps in my child's knowledge and skills.

Throughout these 2 years I never saw any 'secret sauce' from the tutor, just diligent work by my child reflected in good scores over the many Saturday mornings she worked hard across many months. I continued with the tutor's lessons, as I assumed there would be valuable insights my child would gain as she approached the first exams in October Year 6. My assumption, as it turned out, was very wrong.

I got a real shock in September Year 6 just before my child sat her first selective state school exam, which was also her first 11+ exam. After 2 years of work with the tutor, and despite the tutor advertising himself as a specialist in applications for this school, as well as knowing my child was to sit these papers within a few weeks, I had not seen my child spend any time practicing past 11+ papers. I had only seen my child attempt the Bond-type papers that I was marking each week. I reasoned that the tutor knew what he was doing, and must have been parsing past papers during classes.

A month before this first selective school exam, I asked the tutor if my child should do some exam practice at home too with, say, GL Assessment practice papers. The tutor replied, "But I thought you'd already been practising these papers." As this was so close to the first exam, I suddenly felt the previous 2 years had been a tremendous waste of my child's time and my money.

The time of this 11+ exam came and went. My child sat this exam and my fear was realised: despite the tutor remaining confident my child would definitely pass the exam and be offered a place at this school, my child's application went no further.

B - Creating the 13 week plan

So ahead of sitting selective exams for independent schools in January Year 6, I decided to let the tutor continue to do what he was doing once a week and took full responsibility for preparing my child for the rest of her applications, which were for selective independent schools. I had never wanted to do this before because I was worried it might cut across the tutor's preparations and so confuse my child much more than it might have helped. Besides, I reasoned, what did I know that such an experienced 11+ tutor did not?

After receiving the results of the selective state school exam I gathered past papers from each of the schools my child was planning to apply to (plus those of other well-regarded selective independent schools) and worked out a 13 week schedule that lead up to my child's first exam in January. Why 13 weeks? Because that is the exact time my child had left to prepare before the first exam in January Year 6. 13 weeks to learn valuable exam technique and to practise answering written test questions. Would I have preferred it had been 26 weeks or 52 weeks? At that point, of course I would have been happier with that. But I did not have more than 13 weeks, so a 13 week plan was what I drew up.

During these 13 weeks, my child practised sets of Maths and English past papers over and over again, until she could answer the questions in these papers in the style of, and using the techniques described in, Part II. (For Verbal Reasoning and Non-Verbal Reasoning, my child cycled through 8 sets of GL Assessment papers over and over again.) This repetition over the weeks of the same materials acted to ingrain in my child how to comprehend anything asked by a novel question and sparked in her how to answer these different questions.

It is important always to start this type of repetition with a broad set of papers to highlight weaker areas that must be addressed. This is not trying to 'question spot', rather this is learning fundamental techniques to answer Maths, English, Verb Reasoning and Non-Verbal Reasoning questions by recognising which techniques ought to be used in any novel situation. And this works, but you have to commit to it as otherwise your child will not become familiar enough with recognising different scenarios to apply all the different techniques she will have learned.

Practically, after incorporating what I learned from this process, this is the 13 week schedule I subsequently used for my son and have now reproduced in the framework described in detail in this Part III. It has worked very well for my children, so I feel very happy to present this now for you to use for your child.

3. What to do during the 13 weeks before the first exam

A - Reading 1 hour each day

Assuming your child reads regularly from a broad range of books across a variety of topics, I believe you need a minimum of 4 months to prepare for 11+ exams. The key as I have said above is your child should have been reading a broad range of increasingly difficult books to build general knowledge and vocabulary. The background given by this reading is crucial to the work to be covered in the 13 week timetable ahead of the first exam.

What if your child has not been reading in this way during this 13 week period? Well, then see Chapter 4 above regarding how I believe your child should approach reading. Not reading diligently is the one thing that does make this 13 week programme much harder to succeed with, although still not impossible so long as your child starts to read a lot every day: difficult but possible. Your child will only sit the 11+ exams once, so why not make her make this super effort? Worst case is your child will have read a lot more books doing this than if she does not even give this a go - hardly the worst use of your child's time.

B - What else is to be done

Practising past papers is now key. These are the papers I had asked you to obtain from each of the selective schools your child is applying to. At this stage, it is no longer enough to use Bond-type papers, as these are too easy to complete 3 months before the first exam. Instead, you need to concentrate your child's efforts on the following core activities over the next 4 months:

- Take 1 year of these Maths and English papers and work through each question methodically but not under any time pressure.

- Go over all of the questions and answers from each Maths and English paper one after the other until your child can look at each question and describe to you out loud the detailed approach to structure an answer to each question.

- Repeat this process with the second set of papers from that school.

- Once comfortable with these papers, tackle further sets of papers from other schools using the same approach, again *without* time pressure. Each time you must emphasise the correct approach your child must follow for each question, and how she must take care to set out each answer in a structured way.

This process will of course take many weeks to complete, and will form the backbone of much of your child's 11+ exam preparation.

When answering a question, it is important that your child works carefully to set out each step of the answer in a way that she herself can follow. Structured answers will help your child spot mistakes in her reasoning, allow her to check answers carefully when she is under time pressure in an actual 11+ exam, as well as leading the examiner through her work in an ordered way to maximise her marks from each question she attempts.

If the structuring of answers is done systematically, over time she will build a good understanding of how to approach and answer a broad set of 11+ exam questions. This repertoire of answering different types of questions will drive her effort and resilience when she comes across questions presented in an unfamiliar way.

Further, your child must develop the excellent habit of always **checking** her work. In fact, your child has to believe it is crucial to check her own work. She should do this by following a careful process to second-guess her initial answer each time she answers a question.

- She cannot just rely on her intuition to 'feel' the answer is correct but must believe that she needs to check and correct an answer right away after her initial attempt at the answer. In my experience, intuition is better used to feel how an answer might be *wrong* rather than to feel an answer is definitely correct.

- If the second stab at the answer produces the same answer as the first, she should believe that this means that she is less likely to have made the same mistake twice, but of course still cannot be 100% sure it is definitely correct.

I believe the message that checking is so worthwhile takes the longest to be appreciated and no amount of bribery, lecturing or cajoling will speed this process; she will check only when she sees how valuable it is for her to do so, which she will truly believe only when she sees her scores improving consistently. At which time she will need to learn to keep checking. Making sure she continues to check is probably even more difficult than persuading her to check in the first place; this is an area that needs to be worked on continually.

Moreover, once past papers can be completed and checking is becoming more ingrained in your child's answers, **timing** is the next focus. For this, even as early as the third attempt at completing a timed paper will show good improvement. If you persist with timed practice papers, she will soon grow to feel timing is not a problem and instead will be able to focus better on writing a good answer within a given time. Eventually she will be able to do this without feeling undue time pressure. Almost inevitably, I expect your child will have some setbacks on getting the timing right, but you must persist with this as timing will get better only with practising more papers. However, do leave a week or at least a few days between asking your child to sit practice papers under time pressure, as this will leave some time for your child to think through her approaches and decide which areas she needs to focus on to address any timing problems.

C - The timetable you must follow

Table 9.1 below sets out a detailed weekly description of what your child should do during the seemingly too-short period stretching from 13 weeks before the first exam until 4 weeks after. This short, structured time of 17 weeks includes 4 weeks after the first exam to give your child time to sit other school exams, prepare for second rounds of exams and attend any interviews.

For September/October Year 6 exams, your child will need to begin this 13 week timetable at the beginning of June Year 5 (to allow for a slower pace being likely during the August holiday period). This means that if you decide that ultimately it is valuable for your child to join a tutor's class as well as following this programme, your child can join in January Year 5 to prepare from then. Again, fully expect the tutor to tell you you've left it too late and he will try to do what he can for your child.

Of course during this time your child's current school will still be setting homework for her and making other demands on her time outside the classroom, so you will be asking alot of your child, but it is important to keep up this workrate and in a few weeks it will be over and then she can enjoy the remainder of her Year 6 and the summer!

4. What to do during the 4 weeks after the first exam

After the first exam has been sat, you will need to follow a similar process to cover the remaining exams, the timings of which you will have already mapped out (see Table 1.1 above). But do keep going with the daily reading, so each day your child practises concentrating.

After you have looked through the detail of this 13 week programme, the next chapter gives further detail of what to do during the following 4 week period, including the inter-exam days, e.g. whether or not your child should complete past papers under exam conditions during these days. There is a balance you will need to strike here between believing 'more practise is better' and your child suffering exam fatigue that might cause her to care less during an exam about whether or not she does well than she should care.

5. Preparing your child to sit exams

Following my timetable will prepare your child well in a minimum of 4 months. Not 25 months, as your child would need if she started the 11+ process in January Year 4. Just 4 months.

Although you can change this timetable as you feel comfortable, this has served me very well as I prepared my children well enough that they were able to pass exams set by a range of selective, fee-paying schools before interviewing at them and then accepting offers from selective English Top 10 girls and boys schools.

Of course, I did not sit the 11+ exams, they did, but this programme helped create the right conditions to prepare them well.

Building on the weekly timetable set out in Table 9.1 below, the next chapter contains a detailed daily description of what your child should do during the 2 weeks before the first exam to 4 weeks after, which is clearly the critical time to make sure everything comes together as planned.

Table 9.1. Weekly study plan from Week E-13 to Week E+4

Week	Action
Week E-13	<ul><li>1 hour of reading each day</li><li>Maths: use paper 1 from School 1</li><li>English<ul><li>Comprehension: use paper 1 from School 1</li><li>Composition: use paper 1 from School 1</li></ul></li><li>Verbal Reasoning: understand and apply the different Types of questions</li><li>Non-Verbal Reasoning: understand and apply the different Types of questions</li></ul>
Week E-12	<ul><li>1 hour of reading each day</li><li>Maths: use paper 1 from School 1</li><li>English<ul><li>Comprehension: use paper 2 from School 1</li><li>Composition: use paper 2 from School 1</li></ul></li><li>Verbal Reasoning: understand and apply the different Types of questions</li><li>Non-Verbal Reasoning: understand and apply the different Types of questions</li></ul>
Week E-11	<ul><li>1 hour of reading each day</li><li>Maths: use paper 2 from School 1</li><li>English<ul><li>Comprehension: use paper 1 from School 2</li><li>Composition: use paper 1 from School 2</li></ul></li><li>Verbal Reasoning: understand and apply the different Types of questions</li><li>Non-Verbal Reasoning: understand and apply the different Types of questions</li></ul>

Week E-10	• 1 hour of reading each day
	• Maths: use paper 2 from School 1
	• English
	    o Comprehension: use paper 2 from School 2
	    o Composition: use paper 2 from School 2
	• Verbal Reasoning: understand and apply the different Types of questions
	• Non-Verbal Reasoning: understand and apply the different Types of questions

Week E-9	• 1 hour of reading each day
	• Maths: use paper 1 from School 2
	• English
	    o Comprehension: use paper 1 from School 3
	    o Composition: use paper 1 from School 3
	• Verbal Reasoning: understand and apply the different Types of questions
	• Non-Verbal Reasoning: understand and apply the different Types of questions

Week E-8	• 1 hour of reading each day
	• Maths: use paper 2 from School 2
	• English
	    o Comprehension: use paper 2 from School 3
	    o Composition: use paper 2 from School 3
	• Verbal Reasoning: understand and apply the different Types of questions
	• Non-Verbal Reasoning: understand and apply the different Types of questions

Week E-7	• 1 hour of reading each day
	• Maths: use paper 1 from School 3
	• English
	    o Comprehension: use paper 1 from School 4
	    o Composition: use paper 1 from School 4
	• Verbal Reasoning: understand and apply the different Types of questions
	• Non-Verbal Reasoning: understand and apply the different Types of questions

Week E-6	• 1 hour of reading each day • Maths: use paper 2 from School 3

	- English
	    - Comprehension: use paper 2 from School 4
	    - Composition: use paper 2 from School 4
	- Verbal Reasoning: understand and apply the different Types of questions
	- Non-Verbal Reasoning: understand and apply the different Types of questions

Week E-5	- 1 hour of reading each day
	- Maths: use paper 1 from School 4
	- English
	    - Comprehension: use paper 1 from School 1
	    - Composition: use paper 1 from School 1
	- Verbal Reasoning: understand and apply the different Types of questions
	- Non-Verbal Reasoning: understand and apply the different Types of questions

Week E-4	- 1 hour of reading each day
	- Maths: use paper 2 from School 4
	- English
	    - Comprehension: use paper 2 from School 1
	    - Composition: paper 2 from School 1
	- Verbal Reasoning: understand and apply the different Types of questions
	- Non-Verbal Reasoning: understand and apply the different Types of questions

Week E-3	- 1 hour of reading each day
	- Maths: review the hardest paper worked on to date
	- English
	    - Comprehension: review all papers done so far
	    - Composition: review all papers done so far
	- Verbal Reasoning: review all papers done so far
	- Non-Verbal Reasoning: review all papers done so far

Week E-2	- 1 hour of reading each day
	- Maths: see Table 10.1
	- English
	    - Comprehension: see Table 10.1
	    - Composition: see Table 10.1

	- Verbal Reasoning: see Table 10.1
- Non-Verbal Reasoning: see Table 10.1
Week E-1	- 1 hour of reading each day
- Maths: see Table 10.1
- English
- Comprehension: see Table 10.1
- Composition: see Table 10.1
- Verbal Reasoning: see Table 10.1
- Non-Verbal Reasoning: see Table 10.1
E-day	- 1 hour of reading each day
- Maths: see Table 10.1
- English
- Comprehension: see Table 10.1
- Composition: see Table 10.1
- Verbal Reasoning: see Table 10.1
- Non-Verbal Reasoning: see Table 10.1
Week E+1	- 1 hour of reading each day
- Maths: see Table 10.1
- English
- Comprehension: see Table 10.1
- Composition: see Table 10.1
- Verbal Reasoning: see Table 10.1
- Non-Verbal Reasoning: see Table 10.1
Week E+2	- 1 hour of reading each day
- Maths: see Table 10.1
- English
- Comprehension: see Table 10.1
- Composition: see Table 10.1
- Verbal Reasoning: see Table 10.1
- Non-Verbal Reasoning: see Table 10.1
Week E+3	- 1 hour of reading each day
- Maths: see Table 10.1
- English
- Comprehension: see Table 10.1
- Composition: see Table 10.1
- Verbal Reasoning: see Table 10.1
- Non-Verbal Reasoning: see Table 10.1

Week E+4	<ul><li>1 hour of reading each day</li><li>Maths: see Table 10.1</li><li>English<ul><li>Comprehension: see Table 10.1</li><li>Composition: see Table 10.1</li></ul></li><li>Verbal Reasoning: see Table 10.1</li><li>Non-Verbal Reasoning: see Table 10.1</li></ul>

Chapter 10 - The Final Stretch: Week E-2 to Week E+4

1. Preparations during the final Six Weeks

You now really are in the home straight of this marathon as your child heads towards the first exam. It is now all about your child putting into effect all of her preparation and hours working through practice papers. For this you need a detailed, daily plan for your child rather than hoping for the best that everything comes together on each exam day.

Table 10.1 below sets out a daily plan covering the final 2 weeks leading up to the first exam plus the 4 weeks following it. This 6 week plan describes what you should do and when. These are practical, granular actions for each day that will continue to build the momentum of your child's progress, and provide the platform for her to do well.

I cannot emphasise enough this is not the time to abandon the plan you will have worked to for months. Do not lose *your* nerve. This is your child's time to do the best she can. If she has prepared as planned and practised past papers as I have described above, you must take care not to distract her with your worries over these final weeks.

Unless you have been through this process before (and even if you have, this time is with a different child, so it is very likely to be different), it is quite possible that you will not believe your child has done enough to pass her 11+ exams. It is critical that your assumptions and biases (whether negative or positive) do not detract from, or even spoil, what your child is capable of doing over these final 6 weeks. Of course, despite all of this work, there is certainly no guarantee that she will receive even a single offer from a selective school, but is that any reason for your child not to try to approach each exam as prepared and focused as possible?

You have to trust that your child has prepared as well as she can, and now it is about concentrating on completing the race with good form rather than you feeling that you need to scramble to get your child over the finish line anyway that you can. She needs your support to finish this process strongly, so do not get too excited if your child says she does well on an exam or too disheartened if she explains she did not finish a paper. Your role here is neither Chief Cheerleader nor to be despondent at every turn.

Instead, persuade your child gently but firmly that she should stay calm and finish the job well.

Your child is sitting the exam papers, so it is up to her to put everything into practice. You are one of her key sources of strength and should be metronomically reminding her of the best things to do when she is sitting an exam paper. By now she will draw comfort from feeling she can sensibly attempt any question asked in any of the subjects, or have good enough exam technique to know what to do if something unexpected does come along, which of course will happen.

All of this time you thought you were teaching to sit 11+ exams, but really you have been teaching your child the importance of persistent effort and resilience; the interviews will give her plenty of opportunities to demonstrate her empathy.

2. The daily plan

Using the information you have collected so far, map out on a copy of the daily chart detailed in Table 10.1 when each exam will be sat to get a clear sense of exam spacing and the time available in-between them to finalise preparing for them. Triple-check that these timings are accurate and will not change at the last minute just because you had not noted the timings carefully enough. Otherwise you are risking unnecessary stress for your well-prepared child just because you have not prepared properly.

Of course, feel free to alter table 10.1 for your child in order to take into account what in your judgment are your child's needs by modifying the recommended timetable. Remember you are responsible, but also please appreciate that this timetable has been drawn up with careful thought.

Until all the exam papers have been sat and this 6 week period has ended, keep to an absolute minimum any regular extra-curricular activities that your child would usually engage with. Having said that, it is still useful in my opinion to keep a single once-a-week activity session that she has been doing for some time. This will act to provide a sense of familiar structure to these weeks without interfering to any great extent with valuable preparatory time, e.g. a weekly activity such as a weekly sports session each Sunday or weekly drama lessons on a Saturday. Certainly, do not start anything new, which might introduce a potential distraction in these last few weeks. It is best that your child experiences familiar feelings during this time to help her stay calm as the date of the first exam approaches ("E-day").

3. Day E-2

On the day that is 2 days before the first exam (i.e. Day E-2), run through a paper for each subject that your child will sit on E-day. I would expect these to be timed papers, and the feeling of this time pressure will stay with her on E-day. I believe this is a very useful exercise for your child: if these timed papers are a breeze, then it will give her confidence ahead of E-day, but if her timings are off for these papers, the practice even at this late stage will still help.

Remember that E-day is the date of only the first exam and you need to be mindful of doing what is best to also help your child do her best in the other exams that follow. Further, if the pressure of timed papers highlight areas to look at further, it is of course much better to be able to address any such issue even with 2 days to go rather than hope these questions do not turn up again so that you can assume everything will be alright on E-day.

Although you might feel timed exams might be too much for your child to bear so close to the first exam, you should be careful this is not really about you feeling uncomfortable. You need to be quite disciplined to do what makes most sense for your child.

Also, on this day make sure you review quickly with your child past tricks and difficult areas in each subject, as well as continuing with the daily 1 hour of reading.

4. Day E-1

On day E-1 (i.e. the day before the first exam), do a light run-through of all the subjects being sat in the first exam. Your child has to feel the first exam is important and not just another iteration of the seemingly endless cycles of timed practice papers. Do not do timed papers today where timed practice papers have been sat over the previous 2-3 days, unless there has been a problem and you believe it is absolutely necessary to do more timed practise today. Even then do not ask your child to sit a full set of papers.

For each subject you do need to be careful to do the following:

- English:

    o Comprehension: review again the general P-E-E approach and how this acts as an internal check on the consistency of the argument being set out in a comprehension answer. Walk through approaches to past types of questions you have discussed with your child and how to approach those that stumped her then.

    o Composition: review the general framework for writing stories (especially descriptive stories). Your child should read through her past attempts focusing on how the quality of the stories has developed over time. In particular, write out a timed plan, and then review the structure and content of that and past plans, as well as essays written during the weeks of 11+ preparation. Much of this will stick in your child's mind for tomorrow.

- Maths: review past exam papers completed to make sure techniques are refreshed, and review the tricks that you have come across during your child's preparation.

- Verbal Reasoning: walk through an untimed GL Assessment paper and review tricks identified on past Verbal Reasoning papers.

- Non-Verbal Reasoning: do the same as for Verbal Reasoning.

Also, every day your child still needs to do an hour of reading to keep her engaged in her exam mode and concentrating for 1 hour bursts.

5. E-day

After months of preparation, you and your child have arrived at the morning of her first exam. So what should you do in these couple of hours? Do NOT wake your child early to cram. Your child should be well-fed (give her whatever she normally asks for breakfast), and together you should look through a couple of pages of distilled notes to remind her of some common, basic techniques, such as dividing fractions and P-E-E, but say again to your child that she must:

> *"read everything carefully, ignoring whatever else is happening in the room"*

and

> *"check carefully as you go through the different parts of a question – if something looks very easy, check very carefully that you have not missed an alternative, better interpretation as it is unlikely that an 11+ question will be very straightforward".*

After the first exam, do not do any more studying this day, but do read for an hour in the evening.

6. After E-day

You will have already mapped the timing of each subsequent exam, so repeat the same process ahead of each remaining exam, namely:

- on the day before that exam, do a light review of all papers being sat the following day (especially things to watch out for); and

- on each day before that and since the previous exam, do untimed walkthroughs of a paper for each subject to be sat during the next exam.

Unless timing was a real problem on the first exam (unlikely, given the practise so far, but possible), do no more timed papers unless there is a break of a 5 or more days between successive exams. The actual exams should provide adequate acclimatization to exam conditions, so it is better for your child to spend reiterating connections already made during her preparation over the past months.

Rather than looking at reams of notes during the time before the next exam, it is better to adopt a structured approach by going over past exam questions and asking your child to walk through the questions with you orally and testing her by changing some of the facts so her understanding is more robust of the techniques and the relationships between them, e.g. if she is happy with dividing 2 vulgar fractions, make one or both of the fractions mixed or ask her to add or subtract the fractions instead.

Remember to keep up with the daily 1 hour of reading as this will give continuity to the whole process, continue to build vocabulary and practise the daily discipline of sitting down for 1 hour at a time, i.e. slightly longer than the length of 1 exam paper.

7. Daily study plan for these 6 weeks

Table 10.1 below sets out a detailed daily description of what your child should do during the 2 weeks (E-14 days) before the first exam to 4 weeks (E+28 days) after.

Table 10.1. Daily study plan from Day E-14 to Day E+28

Day	Action
Day E-14 (Week E-2)	• Untimed walk through of most difficult past Maths paper available • 1 hour of reading
Day E-13 (Week E-2)	• Untimed walk through of Maths paper from E-14 • 1 hour of reading
Day E-12 (Week E-2)	• 1 hour of reading • Rest of the day off
Day E-11 (Week E-2)	• 1 hour of reading • Rest of the day off
Day E-10 (Week E-2)	• 1 hour of reading • Rest of the day off
Day E-9 (Week E-2)	• 1 hour of reading • Rest of the day off
Day E-8 (Week E-2)	• 1 hour of reading • Rest of the day off

Day E-7 *(Week E-1)*	• Untimed walk through of VR and NVR GL Assessment papers • 1 hour of reading
Day E-6 *(Week E-1)*	• Untimed walk through of Maths and English papers from E-13 • 1 hour of reading
Day E-5 *(Week E-1)*	• Untimed walk through of Maths and English papers from E-6 • 1 hour of reading
Day E-4 *(Week E-1)*	• Untimed walk through of Maths paper from E-5 • 1 hour of reading
Day E-3 *(Week E-1)*	• Timed papers for each subject to be sat on E-day • 1 hour of reading
Day E-2 *(Week E-1)*	• Untimed walk through of all papers to be sat on E-day • 1 hour of reading
Day E-1 *(Week E-1)*	• Light review of a paper for each subject being sat on E-day • 1 hour of reading
E-day	• First school's exam today • 1 hour of reading
Day E+1 *(Week E+1)*	• Untimed walk through of all papers to be sat on E+3 • 1 hour of reading
Day E+2 *(Week E+1)*	• Light review for all papers being sat tomorrow • 1 hour of reading
Day E+3 *(Week E+1)*	• Sit second school's exam today (this timing is assumed to illustrate planning after the previous exam) • 1 hour of reading
Day E+4 *(Week E+1)*	• Untimed walk through of all papers to be sat on E+7 • 1 hour of reading
Day E+5	• Untimed walk through of all papers to be sat

(Week E+1)	on E+7
	• 1 hour of reading
Day E+6 *(Week E+1)*	• Light review for all papers being sat tomorrow
	• 1 hour of reading
Day E+7 *(Week E+1)*	• Sit third school's exam today (this timing is assumed to illustrate planning after the previous exam)
	• 1 hour of reading
Day E+8 *(Week E+2)*	• Untimed walk through of all papers to be sat on E+11
	• 1 hour of reading
Day E+9 *(Week E+2)*	• Untimed walk through of all papers to be sat on E+11
	• 1 hour of reading
Day E+10 *(Week E+2)*	• Light review for all papers being sat tomorrow
	• 1 hour of reading
Day E+11 *(Week E+2)*	• Sit fourth school's exam today (this timing is assumed to illustrate planning after the previous exam)
	• **No reading today.**
Day E+12 *(Week E+2)*	• 1 hour of reading
Day E+13 *(Week E+2)*	• 1 hour of reading
Day E+14 *(Week E+2)*	• 1 hour of reading
Day E+15 *(Week E+3)*	• Interview today (this timing is illustrative)
	• 1 hour of reading
Day E+16 *(Week E+3)*	• 1 hour of reading
Day E+17 *(Week E+3)*	• 1 hour of reading
Day E+18 *(Week E+3)*	• Interview today (this timing is illustrative)
	• 1 hour of reading
Day E+19 *(Week E+3)*	• 1 hour of reading

Day E+20 *(Week E+3)*	• 1 hour of reading
Day E+21 *(Week E+3)*	• 1 hour of reading
Day E+22 *(Week E+4)*	• 1 hour of reading
Day E+23 *(Week E+4)*	• 1 hour of reading
Day E+24 *(Week E+4)*	• 1 hour of reading
Day E+25 *(Week E+4)*	• Interview today (this timing is illustrative) • 1 hour of reading
Day E+26 *(Week E+4)*	• 1 hour of reading
Day E+27 *(Week E+4)*	• 1 hour of reading
Day E+28 *(Week E+4)*	• Interview today (this timing is illustrative) • 1 hour of reading

Chapter 11 - Are We There Yet?

We are not yet there. Once the last exam has been sat, and if your child has done as well as she had planned to do, there will be interviews to prepare for, so still much to do.

You need to ensure your child is prepared for each potential interview in case she is called. Notice of an interview may be as short as a couple of days, although schools are increasingly trying to set aside particular dates, which will help with your planning and also avoids the potential for a clash of interviews held by different schools that your child applied to.

1. 11+ process is about reaching and passing the interview stage

In many ways, the whole of the 11+ process is about its final hurdle: securing interviews with your child's preferred schools. On the whole, a school interviews more children than it can possibly offer a place to, so passing a school's 11+ exam is not anywhere near the last step in being accepted by a school. But your child needing to have done 'well enough' in her exams to be called for interview is a necessary step.

What will determine your child being called for interview? The short answer is whatever combination of the following a school thinks is appropriate in respect of your child:

- 11+ exam performance;

- Year 5 school report;

- the school's assessment of the potential of your child; and

- anything else the school might believe to be important. e.g. will your child help fill the new concert hall or use the sparkling rugby pitch by participating in extra-curricular activities offered by that school, as well as work hard academically?

While a selective state school will usually offer places in accordance with your child's performance in the 11+ exam and then on published criteria, such as distance from a child's home to that school, in truth, each selective independent school has very broad, unaudited discretion to admit whosoever that particular school really would like to.

It will sound trite but it is important to remember that the vast majority of selective schools are looking for coach-able, cheerful, relatively articulate children with relatively legible handwriting who will make the most of the facilities and opportunities available at that school. Sure, not everyone will be a County-standard cricketer, but will your child join in enthusiastically with the other pupils whether as part of the Fifth Team or the First Team? Many schools have spent much money over the past couple of decades improving gyms, sports pitches, swimming pools and theatres, so the pressure is on them to make sure they are used fully and have not been built only to support the First Team's efforts.

2. What to do at an interview

If your child has not experienced an interview before, explain to her carefully what to expect and what to do:

- arrive for the interview in plenty of time;

- when your child meets the interviewer, she should make eye contact and smile. Put her hand out for a firm handshake with the interviewer;

- sit down when invited to by the interviewer;

- your child should sit up straight and not slouch during the interview;

- answer each question politely using P-A (rather than the P-E-E your child learned for English comprehension), i.e. make a Point in answer to a question then Amplify the answer with at least 1 reason;

- if your child does not understand a question or did not hear it properly, say 'Would you repeat that, please?'. The interviewer is unlikely to be trying to make the situation stressful so will repeat as asked;

- before answering, pause and think what you want to say. Then say it;

- make sure your child has one or two questions to ask the interviewer when invited to do so. These questions are more likely to be of the 'what's lunch like' type rather than in-depth discussions on academic league table; and

- at the end of the interview, stand up when the interviewer does and then when you leave the interviewer (whether that's in the room or when the interviewer has brought your child back to you) your child should say "Thank you" and shake hands again.

3. What they will ask at an interview

Your child will not know which questions will be asked at a school interview, so preparing for a core set of questions is the best use of her time.

Interviews at selective independent schools are typically either a single interview 20 minutes long or perhaps 2x10 minute interviews. They comprise anything from a general discussion on current affairs to the child's hobbies; from what the child is looking forward to doing at the school to a couple of Maths or English comprehension questions that need to be discussed orally.

How do you prepare your child for such a diverse range of potential topics? The vast majority of interview questions are likely to be covered by the following broad headings:

- School-related questions;

- Hobbies and interests (including sport, music and creative talents, and other extra-curricular activities;

- Current affairs and general knowledge; and

- Questions to ask the Interviewer.

Appendix C sets out a list of potential questions broadly under these headings. Thinking about these questions will help her be more familiar with the feel of an interview and so help her to be more comfortable dealing with any surprising questions. It should be clear to you that these questions should be prepared rather than bluffed through at the last minute. In fact, why aim to bluff? After all, knowing how to approach an answer to these and similar questions is of real benefit to any child, as it will at a minimum make her more curious about the general world, which might seem precocious when they are 10 years old but pretty common when she is aged 13. If now is not the right age for her to discuss these topics, why are just another couple of years much more reasonable?

Moreover, having to think through answers to the questions in Appendix C will help your child to think through the pros and cons of the different schools, and which school she prefers.

4. What if your child is not invited to interview?

It is true that there will be a small but finite chance that your child does well in the exams yet receives no invitation to interview. Selective independent schools are not obliged to publish the results of their 11+ exams, so selectively calling applicants for interview gives the school pretty much as much discretion as it would like to choose whoever it wants to make an offer to. Since most schools do not offer a place to anyone it has not already interviewed then you can see why securing interviews is the final necessary-but-not-sufficient hurdle of the 11+ process. Impress at the interview and your child will likely close in on an offer, although again this is not guaranteed.

This is the essence of why it is clear the 11+ process is not just about being able to pass an exam. So long as your child still has the possibility of receiving an invitation to interview, your child must be prepared well to attend an interview on only a few days' notice.

5. After the interviews what else can there be?

I believe actively promoting intellectual curiosity is one of the real benefits for your child of the 11+ exam process (or indeed any process of systematic learning). An intellectually curious person wants to know why things are the way they are.

As she grows older, it is very easy for parents to assume a child's curiosity will continue to develop, but unless you act to help her develop it, is it not more likely that she might become increasingly self-conscious about displaying her knowledge too openly? It is easy for her to feel she does not want to draw too much attention to herself by being seen as too clever, where when she was a toddler almost everything she did was greeted with applause. What can a parent do? Encouraging her to read a broad range of material is a great start and then discussing with you the ideas she comes across.

Which ideas should your child investigate? The ones that interest her, and she should approach each fresh topic with equal seriousness. Of course not every question will be as large as 'why are we here?', but your intellectually curious child should have the capacity and inclination to ask questions that reveal more granularity, and perhaps the bedrock, behind any idea she finds intriguing.

The key benefit of the 13 week programme set out in this book is that it can be tailored for other exam processes in the future. This will help your child to set goals then produce careful plans of how to work towards them methodically and purposefully.

APPENDICES

Appendix A - Selection of Practice Books

Name	Level	Maths	English	Verbal Reasoning	Non-Verbal Reasoning
Bond Assessment Papers	Year 4 (8-9 years)	✓	✓	✓	✓
Bond Assessment Papers - Book 1	Year 5 (9-10 years)	✓	✓	✓	✓
Bond Assessment Papers - Book 2	Year 5 (9-10 years)	✓	✓	✓	✓
Bond Assessment Papers - Book 1	Year 6 (10-11 years)	✓	✓	✓	✓
Bond Assessment Papers - Book 2	Year 6 (10-11 years)	✓	✓	✓	✓
Bond Assessment Papers (MCQ) - Pack 1	Year 6 (10-11 years)	✓	✓	✓	✓
Bond Assessment Papers (MCQ) - Pack 2	Year 6 (10-11 years)	✓	✓	✓	✓

GL Assessment - Official 11+ Practice Tests (MCQ) - Pack 1	Year 6 (10-11 years)	✓	✓	✓	✓
GL Assessment - Official 11+ Practice Tests (MCQ) - Pack 2	Year 6 (10-11 years)	✓	✓	✓	✓
Other:	Year 6 (10-11 years)	Robson - Maths for Topic Practice & Revision (Books 1-4)	AE Publications - Spelling and Vocabulary (Books 3-10)	Walsh - 9-10 years (Books 1-3)	-

Appendix B - Suggested Reading List

This suggested list of authors and books is a guide to the appropriate level that your child should be reading to ahead of 11+ exams. No-one will expect your child to have read all of these books before sitting 11+ exams. Instead, this list offers suggestions that will encourage your child to read a broad range of interesting books, which will help to build her vocabulary and general knowledge, as well as exploring rich themes.

It is also important that you do not restrict your child to just these or similar materials: as well as fiction, your child should also read a range of other materials including non-fiction, magazines and newspapers.

David Almond	Skellig
Anna Sewell	Black Beauty
Anne Holm	I Am David
Anthony Horowitz	Alex Rider series
Arthur Conan Doyle	Sherlock Holmes
Arthur Ransome	Swallows and Amazons series
Beverley Naidoo	The Other Side of Truth
Brothers Grimm	Complete Grimm Fairy Tales
C. S. Lewis	The Lion, the Witch and the Wardrobe
Charles Dickens	A Christmas Carol
Charles Kingsley	The Water Babies
Charlotte Bronte	Jane Eyre
Clive King	Stig of the Dump
Cornelia Funke	Inkheart trilogy

Daniel Defoe	Robinson Crusoe
Douglas Adams	The Hitchhiker's Guide to the Galaxy
E. Nesbit	The Railway Children
E.B. White	Charlotte's Web
Elizabeth Goudge	The Little White Horse
Eoin Colfer	Artemis Fowl series
Erich Kästner	Emil and the Detectives
Eva Ibbotson	The Star of Kazan
Frances Hardinge	Fly by Night
George Orwell	Animal Farm
Gerald Durrell	My family and Other Animals
Geraldine McCaughrean	The Kite Rider
H.G Wells	The War of the Worlds
Hans Christian Andersen	Fairy Tales
Holly Black	The Spiderwick Chronicles
Ian Serraillier	The Silver Sword
J.K. Rowling	Harry Potter series
J.R.R Tolkein	The Hobbit
Jack London	White Fang
Jamila Gavin	Coram Boy
Jenny Nimmo	Children of the Red King
Joan Aiken	Wolves of Willoughby Chase
Johanna Spyri	Heidi
John Boyne	Boy in the Striped Pyjamas
John Steinbeck	The Pearl
Jonathan Swift	Gulliver's Travels
Jules Verne	Around the World in 80 days
Kate DiCamillo	The Miraculous Journey of Edward Tulane
Keith Gray	Ostrich Boys
Kenneth Graham	The Wind in the Willows
Lee Trenton Stewart	The Mysterious Benedict Society and the Perilous Journey

Lemony Snicket	A Series of Unfortunate Events
Lewis Carroll	Alice in Wonderland
Louisa May Alcott	Little Women
Lucy Montgomery	Anne of Green Gables
Malorie Blackman	Noughts and Crosses
Mark Haddon	The Curious Incident of the Dog in the Night Time
Mark Twain	The Adventures of Huckleberry Finn
Mary Norton	The Borrowers
Melvin Burgess	The Ghost Behind the Wall
Michael Morpurgo	War Horse
Nigel Hinton	Buddy
Nina Bawden	Carrie's War
Philip Pullman	Dark Materials trilogy
Philipa Pearce	Tom's Midnight Garden
Richard Adams	Watership Down
Roald Dahl	Charlie and the Chocolate Factory
Robert Louis Stevenson	Treasure Island
Robert Westall	The Machine Gunners
Rosemary Sutcliffe	The Eagle of the Ninth
Rudyard Kipling	Jungle Book
Susan Coolidge	What Katy Did Next
T.H. White	The Sword in the Stone
Ted Hughes	The Iron Man
Terry Deary	The Fire Thief Fight Back
William Golding	Lord of the Flies
Yan Martel	The Life of Pi

Appendix C - Interview Questions

1. **School-related questions**

- Why are you interested in this school?
- Which other schools are you applying to?
- Which one would you like to go to? Why?
- What is good about this school?
- What could you contribute to this school?
- Is there anything you do not like about this school? Do not list things
- What do you like about your primary school? What do not you like about it?
- What's your behaviour like at school?
- How would your teacher describe you? How would your friends?
- What are you missing at school in order to be at this interview today?
- What are your favourite subjects?
- What do you read?
- What's your favourite book?
- What are you reading right now?

2. **Hobbies and Interests (including sport, music and creative talents, and other extra-curricular activities)**

- What are your hobbies and interests? (Do not say playing computer games or watching TV)
- Which sports do you play? With which teams and levels?
- Why did you start playing the violin/trombone/clarinet/piano? Have you done any grade exams?
- Have you been in any plays?
- What other extra-curricular activities do you do?
- What's your greatest achievement?

3. **Current affairs, general knowledge and other questions**

- What's been happening in the World this week?
- What do you think about climate change/terrorism/other issues?
- Read a passage and answer questions on it.

- Look at this picture / painting. How does it make you feel?
- What does the captain do in a sports team?
- If you could be anyone for a day, who would you be?
- If money were no object, what would you do with it?
- If an alien came to your school and he could only study 1 subject, which subject would you recommend? Why?

4. **Do you have any questions to ask the Interviewer?**

The 11 year old should ask questions important to her rather than what she can have read in the school prospectus.

- What happens during a usual school day/week?
- How much homework is given out every night?
- How do you get help with homework if you need it?
- What happens if I get lost during my first week?

- What's the food like?
- What does everyone do when it rains?
- How do the older children treat Year 7s when they first start at this school?

Printed in Great Britain
by Amazon